D0727706

LEO CULLEN

A Captain's Story

LEO CULLEN

A Captain's Story

Leo Cullen

Irish Sports Publishing

Published by Irish Sports Publishing
Unit 11, Woodview Court,
Tandy's Lane
Lucan, Co Dublin
Ireland
www.irishbooksandauthors.com

First published, 2011

Copyright © Leo Cullen, 2011

The moral right of the author has been asserted.

All rights reserved.

Without limiting the rights under copyright reserved above,
no Without limiting the rights under copyright reserved above,
no part of this publication may be reproduced, stored in or introduced
into a retrieval system, or transmitted in any form or by any means
(electronic, mechanical, photocopying, recording or otherwise)
without the prior written permission of the publisher of this book.

A CIP record for this book is available from the British Library

ISBN 978-0-9563598-7-2

Printed in Ireland with Print Procedure Ltd
Layout and typesetting: Paul McElheron & Associates
Cover Design: Jessica Maile
Photographs: Inpho Sports Agency
and Leo Cullen's personal collection
Front and Back cover images: Inpho Sports Agency

Contents

In memory of Maureen,
who always took such special care of me.

ACKNOWLEDGMENTS

I hadn't thought about writing a book on the 2011 Heineken Cup, or any book for that matter, so my first thanks must go to Liam Hayes who approached me about this project. I've found the process very enjoyable, so Liam thank you for your time and patience as I rambled through my thoughts these past months. To all the team at Irish Sports Publishing, along with Billy and Dan at Inpho, and David Powell, a big thanks.

From Father Corry, one of my first rugby coaches in Willow Park, to Vincent Costello, my coach at SCT level, I'd like to thank all the coaches and volunteers inside the gates of Blackrock College who helped us and devoted so much of their time to helping us develop our love for this great game.

To my parents, Frank and Paula, who have travelled all around the world to support me, I owe you perhaps the biggest thanks of all. Without your support, encouragement and advice I would not have achieved the things I had dreamed of. To my sister, Sarah, and brother, Owen, thank you for all the good memories!

To my wife, Dairine, thank you for your patience and understanding through my ups and downs of what constitutes a 'rugby season'. You understand me better than anyone. Our Wedding Day was a fitting conclusion to an amazing journey.

Without the help of the coaches, fitness staff, medical staff and everyone who works so hard behind the scenes at Leinster Rugby, this story would never have been possible. Thanks to everyone, in particular our manager, Guy Easterby, and head coach, Joe Schmidt, who have also been incredibly supportive of the book.

To the Leinster supporters and all the Leinster families out there –

your support gives us such a lift and makes every match day so special for those of us lucky enough to be involved. Everyone appreciates what you bring to Leinster and we hope to share lots more special days with you.

Finally, to my team-mates, with whom I had the privilege of travelling on this journey. The 2010-11 season was incredible, I'll never forget it. I don't think any of us will.

Thank you.

Leo Cullen

Half time
Heineken Cup Final
Millennium Stadium, Cardiff
'Home' dressing room
Saturday, May 21, 2011
5.49pm

Where …
… are
… they?

I'm at the door. Waiting. We've been waiting a long time. We need to get out there.

We've been at this door too long. Half a minute? Longer?

Usually, the TV guys are knocking on the door, sticking their heads around the corner, asking us are we ready.

"Give us a minute, we'll be there in a minute!" That's what we're always telling them.

Where are they?

Come on … let's go!

There's nothing more to say… There's nothing more I want to say…

There's nothing more I want anybody behind me to say.

There's no sign of anybody…

Come on! We're going… We've got to go. Got to go now!

The last ten minutes in here have been like an hour.

Come on!

Feels like we've been at this door for the last ten minutes. There's a mass of bodies at my back… I can feel it. It's building… Bubbling…

We're ready … now!

We're all ready, let's go…

We've got to go… Got to go now!

Still nobody.

"LET'S GO!" I shout.

I pull the door open wide.

Dylan Hartley scored their third try, in the corner.

It went to the TMO.

Jamie and Darce walked by me as Romain Poite was still speaking into his microphone.

"They got it," said Jamie.

The giant scoreboard at the opposite end of the ground looked like the biggest scoreboard I'd ever seen:

LEINSTER 6 : 22 Northampton

We've got to get the ball. We've got to get the ball back. Got to score!

I'm looking at the clock at the far end of the ground as well. It's frozen in time at… **38:27.**

Got to get the ball… Got to score!

38:27… 38:27… 38:27…

I look at Poite. He's fidgetting… Finally, he's got his arm in the air.

Try.

Let's get on with it!

38:31…

We've got time. We'll get a restart… We need to score.

LEINSTER 6 : 22 Northampton

38:35…

Stephen Myler is moving in slow motion… **38:46…** he's got the ball in his hand. He's waiting to take his kick. He's still waiting.

38:56…

Move Myler, move… COME ON… MOVE!

39:01... 39:03... 39:06...
Romain Poite doesn't seem in any great hurry either.
39:09... 39:10...
Ref... You going to let him take all day?
39:11... 39:12... 39:13...
I need the clock to slow down.
Slow down... Slow down... Slow ... down.
Myler places the ball.
Hurry up... Hurry ... up!
39:21... 39:22... 39:23...
LEINSTER 6 : 22 Northampton
We'll kick the ball off... Kick it to Shaggy. He'll win it back... We'll get down their end, get a penalty and there's two scores in it.
39:33... 39:38... 39:39...
Slow...
... slow!
LEINSTER 6 : 22 Northampton
Myler is still waiting.
Waiting.
Waiting.
Looking up at the posts.
Looking down at the ball.
Looking up.
Down.
He's moving! He runs up ... hits it!
39:55...
Looks good ... good ... NO! It comes off the upright.
39:57...
39:58...
39:59...
40:00.
It's over!
Fuck. We've got to get back into the dressing room. Sixteen points – what was that? The scrum... What's wrong? Fuck!

We're back in the dressing room.

Normally, we take the first two minutes to cool down, recover, breathe out the first half, get our heads straightened out. Then, start thinking what we're going to do in the second half.

Ten minutes in the dressing room can be a long time but we're going to need all the time we can get. The lads look bad.

Joe looks calm.

Joe is speaking slowly.

Our scrum has been a total disaster. We've taken a thrashing.

Fuck ... this could be embarrassing.

Keep calm...

Keep ... calm...

Joe looks calm.

Hinesy, Mike Ross and myself are sitting together. We always sit together. Hinesy is on my left, Mike is on my right.

The room is huge, too bloody big. The rest of the lads look far away ... too scattered.

There are long faces opposite me. Hard faces. They look like shit.

What just happened?

I don't know. It's quiet. Joe's talking.

Lads are taking their drinks, energy gels. Iced towels hide some faces.

Nobody wants to talk.

I turn to Mike.

Keep it calm. Stay calm ... stay strong.

"What's going on?" I ask Mike, calmly.

Mike looks back at me, but he doesn't say anything.

Mike is the general of our scrum – he's the specialist, he's the man! Mike knows everything that's going to happen in every single scrum. Mike lives and breathes scrums.

Mike Ross has prepared us for the Northampton scrum. He knows their scrum as well as he knows our scrum. Mike and our scrum coach, Greg Feek, were ready for everything and anything Northampton had in mind.

Calm... Calm...

"What's going on Mike?" I say again.

Sexto's talking. Jonny Sexton and Shane Jennings do more talking in our dressing room than anyone else – everyone likes to hear them talking.

"LISTEN," Jonny shouts. "We were ten points down to Toulouse, AND WE CAME BACK! And they weren't half the team these guys are!"

What? What did Jonny just say?

I feel like I'm smiling, but I know I'm not smiling.

Does Jonny just know what he's said? If Jonny has that right... If Northampton are twice as good as Toulouse and we're losing to Northampton by 16 points, then ... we're really fucked here!

I'm wondering if anyone else has just heard Jonny say what I think I have just heard Jonny say. Nobody appears to have noticed.

Jonny's just got that arse-ways!

I feel like I'm still smiling.

But, Jonny is almost right. We were 11 points up against Munster just a couple of weeks ago and we went out in the second half and stopped playing.

Northampton are going to stop playing. All we've got to do is start playing.

Jonny's dead right. We were 10 points down against Toulouse, and they're twice as good as Northampton and we came back and beat them in the semi-final.

I feel better. Feel calm.

"WE JUST NEED TO HOLD ONTO THE BALL," Joe shouts loudly, but still with absolute calmness, with absolute certainty.

There's no panic in his voice. He's telling everyone to hold onto the ball.

Joe has three messages he wants to get into everyone's heads –

One: He wants everyone to remember that this Heineken Cup final will go down in "folklore".

Two: He wants us to "hold the ball".

Three: He wants us to start making our tackles count and, to do that, he wants us to keep "moving our feet in defence", and stop standing still.

Those are Joe's three messages.

"ALL THE FORWARDS WITH FEEKIE!", orders Joe.

Greg Feek has his laptop in his hand on the far side of the dressing room. We all get over there to Feekie and huddle around him.

Feekie starts speaking slowly. He's measured in his words. He's talking to Cian and Straussy… He's talking to Mike!

The rest of us are listening – we need to know what's gone wrong.

We're huddled around and we can all see what's happening. We think we see what's happening… Feekie is running through all the scrums: Mike is being angled into Hartley every time they have a put-in. On our put-in, we're okay.

We lost one against the head in our own 22 and they scored a try. That looks bad on Feekie's screen, but that was just a freak moment.

The ball had hit off Cian's leg, popped over to their side. A thousand-to-one shot.

But, they're killing us…

They've a good scrum. No, they've a great scrum!

I see myself arguing with the referee. After one of the scrums, I had to slow things down … had to talk to Romain Poite. I had to tell him they were doing something wrong, even though I had no real idea what they were doing. On Feekie's laptop the lads can't hear me and the referee.

We need Cian and Straussy and Mike to do the job out there.

"Get it sorted!" Joe had told Feekie.

Feekie has told Mike what to do, he's told Cian and Straussy and Mike how to sort it.

He showed us all that Northampton were waiting for the pressure to ease and then they were counter-punching. They stand our guys up and they keep pushing.

That's the message from Feekie and that's what I'd told Romain Poite out on the field in the first half.

"They come up and then they're fucking pushing through," I shouted at the referee. But he was having none of it.

He looked at me with his straight face, and said: "Speak to your players … you are coming under pressure!"

Looking at Feekie's laptop, the others can't hear what the referee and myself are saying to one another, but Poite was looking at me as if he wasn't hearing me.

And so, I started to speak more slowly to him. And then – fucking hell – I started to put on a stupid French accent.

I was speaking to him in English with a French accent.

I'm really going to piss him off if I keep talking to him like this ... with my French accent. So, I shut up.

But I knew that Poite was right. We had to deal with what they were doing but, at the same time, I wanted to start Poite thinking that what they were doing might be borderline.

Might be illegal.

I knew there was something wrong. Cian and myself had been pushing against thin air on our side of the scrum. When a scrum stands up, it's nearly always re-set, but Poite was having none of it.

"Allez. ALLEZ!" That's all I could hear him say.

That monster of theirs on the other side of the scrum, Tonga'uiha, seems to be killing Mike. He's hitting on the outside of Mike and Mike is in no-man's land. We can all see that on the screen in Feekie's hands.

They are murdering us out there, and their backs are coming in, whooping and hollering, slapping their front row on their heads and their shoulders.

They think they have us.

Mike needs to keep low and he needs to keep straight. He needs to keep tighter to Straussy. Mike now knows that, too.

He has to sort it out.

"We need to hold the ball."

"We need to score first!"

"HOLD ... THE BALL," I shout.

"Build phases!"

"We've got to hold the ball... HOLD THE BALL!"

I'm calm now. And ready.

That first half passed me by. I was a spectator. We were all spectators. Now I'm ready to get out there.

Northampton will not want to play this second half. They want to start celebrating. They want to start celebrating now.

Joe and the coaches have left the dressing room.

Before the game started Joe had told us, in no uncertain terms, that this game would be remembered forever: "When you meet each other in the streets in years to come, you'll remember this day forever!"

But, before leaving the dressing room, Joe had stepped up his belief in us to a higher level.

"When we come back from this," he stated to everyone sitting around him, "it'll be... FOLKLORE!"

We're ready.

The shock and horror... The panic... The pain – all gone.

Everyone looks good. We're all calm. Everyone's ready. I see that.

Jenno is in for the second half. Before the coaches left, I'd had to sort through our lineout, let the guys know the calls, make sure everyone was on the same page.

"Hold the ball... HOLD THE BALL." I keep repeating myself: "HOLD ... THE ... BALL."

I want the lads to know that we'll win this by doing the simple things right.

"Just hold the ball... Find the holes!"

Jonny is still talking to the lads – everyone likes to hear Jonny's voice.

"This will be remembered ... forever," he shouts, before repeating it: "This will be remembered ... FOREVER!"

Everyone else is talking, too.

I'm looking at everybody, listening, processing everything.

The scrum's sorted. Now, we need to keep the ball. If we score first, we'll win this thing. Toulouse are far better than these guy. Leicester were too good for Northampton a week ago. We're better than Leicester, we can't lose to these guys.

We get into a huddle. Everyone tightens around. Everyone has something to say.

"They'll tire."

"If we hold the ball, we'll tear them apart."

"HOLD THE BALL... HOLD THE BALL."

Everyone's talking.

"We've got the scrum sorted."

"We can score tries."

The lads are excited, anxious, ready.

"HOLD THE BALL."

"They'll stop playing!"

"They'll run out of steam!"

"Hold the ball… HOLD THE BALL… HOLD THE BALL!"

We've been a long time in the dressing room. Time to get out.

We're twice as ready as we were when we left this room for the start of the game. We're ready to start playing. All of the negative thoughts, which we brought back into the room with us ten minutes ago, are long gone.

Then – back when we came into the dressing room – all I could think was that it was going to be pretty grim watching them lifting the cup: Northampton, Heineken Cup champions, all these young English guys, about to lift the Heineken Cup … I could see Hartley holding the cup over his head.

That's going to be bloody hard to watch.

It seems like an hour has passed since I had all those thoughts.

We finish the huddle and I walk to the door.

Everyone's behind me. We're ready to get out there.

Hold the ball… Break them down… Score first!

But there's nobody on the other side of the door. Nobody!

I don't want anybody to say anything more.

Everyone, I know, has the words in their heads… I know that. I can see it on their faces.

I can hear lads behind me talking to one another, repeating Joe's words, and repeating Jonny's words.

I hear those words in my own head.

"THIS WILL BE REMEMBERED … FOREVER!

"THIS WILL BE REMEMBERED …

"FOREVER …

"FOREVER!"

CHAPTER ONE

"HI, I'M JOE SCHMIDT... SEE YOU LATER!"

Joe Schmidt

If I had any money left I'd light a candle to St Francis and ask him if there's any
chance God could be persuaded to perform a miracle on my shoulders.
Or if I had a stamp I could write to Joe Louis and say, Dear Joe, Is there any chance
you could tell me where you got your powerful shoulders even though you were poor?

Extract from *Angela's Ashes*, Frank McCourt (Scribner)

I've been lucky to make a good living playing the game I love but, I suppose,
I haven't been so lucky in only having one 'good' shoulder all my adult life!
My left shoulder has been officially crocked since an afternoon in Blackrock,
in January 1995, when I was seventeen years old, when Blackrock College
were playing CBC. I went to tackle a guy straight after the kick-off. I hit him
hard to put down a marker but it felt as if my arm had detached from my body.
I had just experienced my first shoulder dislocation. I had to leave school every
lunchtime for the next six weeks and report to the Blackrock Clinic for
physiotherapy treatment, which meant that I didn't get back into the 'Rock
team until the semi-final of the Leinster Senior Cup that year, which we won.

I'm now thirty-three years old.

I've had a good rugby career, and I wouldn't look to change very much, if
anything at all, in my fourteen years as a professional rugby player. To be
honest, I've had the time of my life. I've worn the Irish jersey thirty-three times,
and captained my country three times, including the 2011 World Cup finals in
New Zealand when I had the great honour of leading out the Irish team which
defeated Russia in the group stage.

I've been lucky enough to be part of teams which have won almost
everything in club rugby in Europe, including an English Premiership and EDF
Energy Cup with Leicester, and a couple of Celtic League titles and two
Heineken Cups with Leinster. Captaining Leinster to those two Heineken Cup

triumphs have been the two greatest moments of all for me.

This book is my story, and it is also the story of how Leinster commenced the 2010-2011 season with a new coach, with new ideas of how to play the game, and how we safely navigated a 'Pool of Death' in the Heineken Cup group stages, defeated two of the greatest teams there has ever been in the Northern Hemisphere, in Leicester and Toulouse en route to the final, and then staged the most daring comeback that has ever been seen in the Heineken Cup final by fighting back from a 16 points deficit at half time and defeating Northampton by 11 points in the Millennium Stadium in Cardiff.

But first I want to tell you about my left shoulder!

Three times I've had it reconstructed – most recently when I went under the knife of Len Funk in England, in May 2010, for a procedure which goes by the name of 'Bristow-Latarjet', and which is far too detailed and complicated to explain here and now, but, essentially, it was hoped that it would stop the pattern of recent dislocations.

My shoulder has popped out at all sorts of times, and in all the wrong places.

In Edinburgh, the evening before the 2009 Heineken Cup final, there was one such poorly-timed occasion, for example. I was lying on my back stretching on the physio room floor with my arms stretched over my head when, all of a sudden, my shoulder popped. That night, I tossed and turned all night long, worrying that my shoulder was damaged beyond repair!

There have been too many games in which it has 'gone' and my left arm has been left totally de-powered for several minutes, leaving me to either improvise or quickly think my way through some tricky situations on the field. This shoulder, which all my life I have labelled my 'bad' shoulder, has an assortment of scars as decoration. There's also a metal plate with eight screws in there from when I shattered my collar-bone on that side.

However, apart from that one night in Edinburgh, I've never overly stressed about the shoulder letting me down in games.

I've found that it's best to play the game instinctively and not to worry about what could go wrong. And, most often, in the biggest games I've played in, I've found it easiest to almost forget about my left shoulder entirely.

That said, I occasionally have found myself in situations where I have consciously decided not to dive to my left-hand side to make a tackle, though in the front five on a rugby pitch you are generally in the thick of the action and people you need to tackle or hit are pretty close to you at all times.

Nevertheless, I've got to admit that throughout my adult life I have been getting away with having a crocked left shoulder, more than anything else, through common sense, fast thinking and knowing the game intimately.

In the late spring and early summer of 2010, I thought enough was enough and I needed to have someone else look at my shoulder. In Dublin, my surgeon, Jimmy Colville, had brilliantly put my shoulder back together on two occasions, in 2003 and 2008, and I always received wonderful care and attention from Jimmy and his team. In 95 per cent of cases, one shoulder reconstruction is all it takes to get a player back and feeling as strong as ever. However, my left shoulder was in the 5 per cent of really crocked shoulders.

In May of 2010, I was sitting on the sidelines in the RDS, looking at Leinster lose to the Ospreys in the Magners League final. Michael Cheika had asked me to play in the game.

"Why don't you?" he had asked, suggesting that I postpone my surgery until after the grand final. But, Len Funk had advised me to get the surgery done immediately, and I took his advice.

I knew I wasn't going to be of any use to the team. We'd lost to Toulouse in the most disappointing manner in the semi-final of the Heineken Cup a couple of weeks previously. There's a sense that I bring a certain 'calm' to the team. That's what people seem to think! And we needed a bit of additional calmness at the end of that season. The shoulder had been popping so frequently through the end of the season, however, that there was a good chance it could have gone again after five minutes. Besides, the game was going to be Mal O'Kelly's last for Leinster and I knew that Nathan Hines and Mal would do a better job than I could.

My shoulder was in a sling as I sat on the sideline and the sling remained in place, day and night, for the first three weeks.

But I felt happy.

The road back to full fitness was going to take a full six months, according to Len Funk, but after breaking down so often during the season which was just ending, I was 100 per cent content in my own head that I had given myself a chance of ending my career in the best possible shape for a thirteen-year veteran!

The biggest trouble I'd been in with my shoulder the previous season had been in Twickenham, in late January, when Leinster played London-Irish in a Heineken Cup game which was all about us getting 'revenge' on them for turning us over in the RDS at the beginning of the season in our opening pool game. It popped out, and stayed out. Though I also had another spot of bother in the same game...

Chris Hala'Ufia had given me a box as we scored the first try. I was rucking somebody on the ground, giving him a bit of a shoeing to be honest, when he came in and hit me from the side. It was a good one, to be fair to him! Knocked me flat on my back, and he ended up getting a four-week ban for his troubles. I remember lying on the ground and hearing some noise in the distance. I began to wonder had somebody scored a try?

Late in the second half, they had a lineout and I went to contest it. For some inexplicable reason I reached with my left arm across my body and the shoulder popped. I collapsed on the ground. 'Irish' picked the ball at the back of a ruck and I had Eoin Reddan screaming at me to get up on my feet!

I had my shoulder back in place at that stage, but it was completely de-powered and it was hanging by my side, limp and useless. Play continued and I tried to make a tackle using my good arm. Thankfully, the player went to ground. We were inside our own 22 and, eventually, the ball was kicked up the field, allowing me to make my way over to the sideline.

The strangest thing was, however, despite only having one good shoulder for most of the season, I ended up starting two games for Ireland in the Six Nations – and all I could think of was all the years I'd missed out on selection for Ireland when I had two shoulders which were close enough to being in good working order.

But a shoulder is just a shoulder. You can get by, even at the highest level in the professional game, with a damaged shoulder, whereas with a bad ankle or with a knee which has blown up there's no chance whatsoever.

Besides, I was also tinkering around with all sorts of little things that season, in an effort to give myself every opportunity to play in every game. The day before every game, for example, I did a forty-minute weight session, *usually with one of our coaches, Chris Dennis. It's not normal to do weights the day before a game but, after the light team run, I'd get into some heavy pushing and pulling. I don't know whether that was a good thing or a bad thing but, in my head, it was preparing me for battle. It certainly generated a feeling of power in my arms. It also allowed me to believe that my shoulder was strong.*

We were coming up with all sorts of rehab ideas to give me that extra physical edge I needed. However, all of these additional things I was doing combined to convince me that I was 'mish-mashing' my way through the season. Once there is real damage done to the shoulder, all the rehabilitation in the world is only going to improve the joint by perhaps 10 per cent.

I wanted to have two good shoulders which would see me through to my last game of rugby for Leinster, even if my left shoulder – despite Len Funk's great work – will still remain about 20 per cent weaker than my right shoulder.

My days of running around a rugby field with my left arm dangling uselessly by my side are over, hopefully.

And, not just on the rugby field. A month after winning the Heineken Cup in 2009, I was on a holiday with Dairine and with Shane Jennings and his girlfriend, Cliona, in Croatia, and I found myself in the middle of the sea thinking, God ... what am I up to here?

I'd been on a banana boat.

We were all on the boat and I was holding tightly onto a rope by the side. I don't know what I was doing on the bloody thing in the first place! Next thing, I was thrown off but, as I fell into the water, I tried to hold onto the rope.

My shoulder popped.

I hit the water.

"... Shit!"

I only had power in one arm in the water but the boat stopped so that I could climb back onboard, but I couldn't do it.

As I bobbed up and down in the water, all I really wanted to do was kick myself on the backside. I'd looked after myself all season long, trying to make sure I didn't do too much damage to my left shoulder and ... then ... I got into a banana boat ... and fell out of it!

It's extremely hard, if not impossible, to make a good impression on a new coach when you are recovering from injury.

I didn't expect, or want, any concessions or favours from our new coach and, besides, the beginning of the 2010-11 season wasn't too easy on Joe Schmidt either!

He'd come in and replaced Michael Cheika, or just plain 'Cheiks' to all of us who'd slowly but surely grown to love the man for the strangest reasons, and also due to the simple fact that he'd built the Leinster team from a soft-bellied and under-achieving rugby club into the No. 1 team in Europe by the end of the 2008-09 season.

So, the abrasive, spontaneous, sometimes maddening, often brilliant Aussie exited stage left, and started a new chapter in his life in Paris with Stade Français, and the quietly-spoken, measured Kiwi, who was making no big promises to anybody, entered stage right.

Nothing went right in those first few weeks for Joe. One of the low points of the pre-season was a trip to Leicester when, after an even enough first half, they brought on some experienced players near the end and blew us away. Our 'big names' were coming back in dribs and drabs due to the IRFU's player welfare programme but, when the Magners League kicked off, things didn't get any better. We lost three of our first four games. We had an 11 points victory at home to Cardiff and we got four tries, but we got turned over on the road by Glasgow, Treviso and Edinburgh.

I was 'running the water' during a couple of those games, but I didn't go to Italy as Dairine's sister, Kiera, was getting married that same evening. I was ducking in and out during the wedding meal to get a look at the television set which was showing the game in the Stadio Monigo and, in truth, it was hard to watch. It was wet and miserable in the ground and we looked like pushovers. We were being bullied all over the place. They scored a try in the last minute to make it a 29-13 scoreline at the end.

I was watching all of this unfold, and more than once I thought back to one of the final conversations I'd had with Cheiks, before he left town, when we both agreed that with himself, and Kurt McQuilkin and Alan

Gaffney, leaving the team and with so many senior players retiring – and the IRFU's pre-World Cup welfare programme disrupting team selection – things might unravel for a while during the course of the new season.

I was thinking that this might be one of those seasons... I was also thinking that Joe Schmidt might need to put a three-year plan in front of everybody.

I'd met with Joe Schmidt before he was offered the Leinster job. Jonny Sexton and I sat down with him for about an hour or so, in a city centre hotel, and we found him very interesting company from the very start.

Michael Cheika had decided to move on after spending five years rebuilding the organisation and maybe he felt that his job was done.

The Leinster players didn't want Cheiks' replacement to be some big-shot name with big dreams. We wanted somebody who could give us something definable, something tangible.

We could see by Joe's CV that he's had an incredible amount of experience and his knowledge of the game was second-to-none. He'd been No. 2 to Vern Cotter in Clermont for three years and he'd also been the backs' coach there and had been side by side with Vern as Clermont won the Holy Grail of French rugby, a first Bouclier de Brennus after 99 years of trying. He's got New Zealand Schools, Bay of Plenty and Auckland Blues on his resume as well. He also came highly recommended by Isa Nacewa, who had Joe for three years at the Blues. As Isa is one of the most respected players in the entire squad his advice was good enough for everyone.

Joe and his wife, Kelly, had been here in Ireland before when they spent some time in Mullingar twenty years earlier. He had played with Mullingar, and he was a PE teacher and coach at Wilson's Hospital. But, coming back here to start his first job as Head Coach, leaving the life which he and his four children (Abby, Tim, Ella and Luke) had enjoyed in the Auvergne, was a big step on a professional and a personal level.

He's a smart guy.

Even though our early season results were awful, he had us all thinking and excited about what might lie ahead of us. And, if not in the season commencing, then certainly in future seasons.

Joe sat down with every single player when he took up the job but they were not long, soul-searching conversations. No, they were fast and to the point – much like the manner in which he liked to do everything in the team camp and on the field. Joe is business-like. He likes to get the job done and he likes real-life intensity and full concentration applied to whatever it is he asks us to do.

When I sat down with him, he had me on the back-foot fairly quickly. We were just a minute or two into our talk.

"So, Leo... What are you going to bring to the team this season?" he asked, straight-up.

Just like that!

Thirteen years of being a professional rugby player was of no real importance to Joe, that was clear. He wanted to know what I was going to do for him in the next eight or nine months.

I didn't mind the question.

Actually, I liked it. I could see what he was aiming for at the start of his new relationship with all of the Leinster players, and he was dead right to wipe the slate clean on everything which had occurred in the Leinster camp before he arrived.

But, his questions were damn good. He hit one of our forwards right between the eyes, with one spectacular punch.

"So, if Paul O'Connell saw you walking down the street, what do you reckon he'd be thinking about you?"

Answer that!

My relationship with Michael Cheika had been interesting. We were completely different people, but I believe we had huge respect for one another. He's so complex in many ways, but he's also brilliant. We'd talk all the time, always as coach and captain. But, we'd never chit-chat, we'd never go for a beer, we'd never even think of meeting up socially.

That's because Cheiks wasn't one for a few beers at any time during the season really. He'd prefer to find a place in town which served up a great cup of coffee, and that's where we'd meet if we had to talk through some team business privately.

When Cheiks decided it was time to move on, nobody in Leinster was at all surprised. He was hot property at the time, especially so after just winning the Heineken Cup in 2009, and he still is hot property in European rugby. Everyone in our camp thought that Cheiks probably always wanted to go to Paris. He was a fluent French speaker, he owned a place there, and he never hid his love for the city. That was always an in-house piece of fun amongst the players – Who would Cheiks bring to Paris with him?

When he finally announced that he had signed up with Stade Français, we all wished him well.

I liked Joe's style and approach from day one. You see and hear so many coaches in the professional game and you know that a great majority of them spend most of their daily hours spoofing. Some coaches do drills which have absolutely no point to them whatsoever. But, there is always a point to everything which Joe decides to do. You can immediately see what he is trying to bring to the team.

Joe is all 'Bang... Bang... Bang... DONE!' His aim is to get people in and out of camp, or on and off the field, as fast and as purposefully as humanly possible. His attitude is very similar to what I had experienced with Leicester's coaches, during my two years there.

In those first few weeks with Joe I was sitting back somewhat: watching, listening, doing my rehab and taking it all in. Those first few defeats, even though they were very early in the season, were hard on him! We were 10 points up against Glasgow, but still managed to lose the game, even though we've always found Firhill a dog of a place to visit. Jamie Heaslip had to come off after 60 minutes because of the player management programme, and that didn't help us grind out the win we needed! Losing to Treviso was awful, losing to Edinburgh was worse still!

The Sunday morning after the game in Edinburgh, I called Joe. I wanted him to know for sure that all of the players were 100 per cent behind him and what he was doing. The heat was coming on him in the media, after some of the mixed results in the early season. That was the first and last time I spoke with him to make sure that he still believed in Leinster and in his decision to come to Dublin.

I 100 per cent believed that.

First time Joe had addressed the players as one body, he spent all of fifteen seconds with his pleasantries.

"Hi... I'm Joe Schmidt... I'll try to get to know everyone in the next few weeks. Best of luck... SEE YOU LATER!"

That's the way to do it!

There was no point in someone coming in and trying to 'steam-roll' the camp. It was smarter to assess the situation, and everyone in the situation, first. Joe, in my opinion, is the purest rugby coach, in terms of technique and application, I have ever come across.

Our next game up was against Munster in the Aviva Stadium. It was Leinster's first time in the sparkling new ground. It was also Joe's first meeting with our great rivals, whom we'd beaten on the last four occasions.

Joe asked me to join Jono Gibbes and himself in the coaches' box in the Aviva that Saturday night.

But, it wasn't where I really wanted to be. I didn't like being so far away from the team and it didn't help that people walking past thought they could knock on the window any time they liked!

The captaincy of the team was with Jamie.

Jamie Heaslip always leads by his actions and gets on with it. He's also absolutely clinical in his match preparation. While people seem surprised that he has so many wide and varied interests off the field, Jamie remains the model professional.

Though, he sucker-punched Joe before the Heineken Cup quarterfinal in the RDS at the end of the previous season. Joe and the Clermont lads had completed their warm-up and Joe was standing on the sideline, looking around him, and he was drawn to the 'interesting' spectacle of Jamie and Cian Healy trying to whack some dropped-goals, as they are both prone to do before games. Joe told me that, when he saw them, he thought to himself that Clermont were going to throttle us in the game.

Jamie, of course, did not hit very many goals over the bar during the warm-up, but he scored two tries that evening, and was awarded Man of the Match.

Munster were four wins from four at the beginning of the evening, and they hit their stride in the game pretty quickly.

Nobody in Leinster was thinking of five in a row against Munster. That, believe me, is a game of numbers which is all in the heads of the Irish rugby media. We just want to try to beat Munster every time we meet them, we're not foolish enough to be counting. We needed to beat them that evening but, more importantly, we needed a win over anybody.

Drico's try nailed the 13-9 victory for us near the end, but we had controlled the game for most of the second half. The team's hunger and desire to make the tackles that needed to be made were back in that half. Also back, for twenty-five minutes, was Jonny Sexton and, although he left the kicking to Isa because of a leg strain, his presence poured confidence and self-belief into the whole team.

The Aviva itself looked so slick.

Everything about the place is five-star and the dressing rooms are phenomenal. Winning, and winning in a place which felt as much a home to us as the RDS, was a pivotal moment. It was so important to win. And, in fairness to our supporters, they really bought into the occasion and made the Aviva that evening a special time and place.

I was into my fifth month of rehab.

When I was in the middle of my recovery from surgery I had no doubts about my ability to come back and revert to my role in the team, and my role as team captain. But, the closer I was getting to full fitness, the more I began to question myself and the strength in my shoulder, and also question the exact date of my return.

I was still one month short of the full six-month recovery period which Len Funk and his team had advised.

But, Joe was pushing me to sit on the bench against Racing Metro in the first game of our Heineken Cup campaign. I was pushing myself, too. Originally, I had targetted the game against Munster in the Aviva Stadium as the date of my return but I knew I was not right to rejoin the match squad that weekend.

I was thinking of Racing Metro. Or Saracens the following week. The prospect of playing in Wembley was hugely exciting and compelling for me and for everyone in the squad. Admittedly, I was also thinking about Declan Kidney and the Irish squad, which he would soon be naming for the November International series.

The day after we defeated Munster, I went into Joe's office and told him I was not right, and I couldn't put myself forward for selection for the match 23 for the game against Racing. That was hard. It was bloody hard to go up to our new coach and, effectively, tell him no.

That same day was the day of the Heineken Cup launch in Dublin. For the previous three years the launch had been within a couple of days of Leinster playing Munster in the Magners League. And, on two of those occasions, that had meant me spending the morning with Paul O'Connell, Rory Best, a gaggle of photographers, and most of the country's rugby writers.

I turned up for the launch, once again, as Leinster team captain – and with my head in a bit of a spin from the strangest conversation with Joe!

We'd talked quite a bit at this stage, about bits and bobs, and I'd been straight up with him at all times. But, funny enough, we had never spoken directly about the captaincy of the team.

Who was going to captain Leinster for the 2010-11 season? Jamie was standing in for me, I thought, until I returned to full fitness. However, I was not sure what was in Joe's head.

In the end, the week before the Heineken Cup launch, Joe phoned me and was a little vague about the whole thing.

"Europe are looking for us to put down a captain for the Heineken Cup," he began. "And ... we're going to put your name down. We're not sure how the year is going to go, but we'll put you down for it!" he concluded, matter of factly.

That was Joe.

Business-like, and presenting a clean slate on the captaincy of the Leinster team! That's the way it should have been. Everybody, and everything, was beginning from scratch. All the players wanted it like that.

And I wanted it exactly like that too. We all wanted to start afresh with Joe. Problem was, in my head I originally had no doubts that Joe was going to retain me as team captain. I'm no different than any professional sports person. If I feel I am the best person for a job, then I will back myself 100 per cent.

But, Joe got me thinking.

And then I got thinking about Joe, and I began to wonder was he really considering giving the captaincy to Jamie, or someone else, for good?

I had taken over the job of Leinster captain from Brian O'Driscoll, the year after I had returned to Leinster from Leicester. We were in preseason camp, in Italy, when Cheiks announced me as captain, and Whits and Jenno as vice-captains.

Once it was announced, Brian came over to me immediately and wished me the very best of luck. He could not have been more decent about it and, as things turned out, without the distraction of being Leinster captain that season he had a year of rugby which was his crowning glory.

Before then, I had spent time as Leicester captain and I had captained Leinster while Drico was away with Ireland. I really was looking forward to the responsibility of being Leinster captain and the great honour which comes with that role.

As captain, I like everyone on the team to get on with their jobs. I am certainly not a dictator and I encourage as many voices as possible in the dressing room, though I discourage waffle and noise for the sake of it, and I always try to cut nonsense talk short at the earliest opportunity.

A dominant team leader sometimes stops people voicing their opinions and that can be stifling in a team environment. People have to be comfortable and happy to talk, so I encourage it. My job is to help the entire team to take ownership of what has to be done, and the more people who feel that they own something then the greater is their response on the field, especially at the most pressurised moments.

I try to treat every player in the dressing room with the same level of respect. That's something I learned in Leicester from Martin Corry, who's a great guy. Corry is someone who brings a hard edge consistently to everything he does within the team grouping. He never needed to say all that much. He knew that less was always more when it came to talk in the Leicester dressing room, and that is my philosophy exactly.

When I was named Leinster captain, however, I was just back from surgery on my shoulder and then, unbelievably, in our second European game that season I broke my collar-bone. Thankfully, we managed 10 points in those first two games which gave us much-needed breathing space later in the group.

The first year I had turned up as Leinster captain for the Heineken Cup launch, we had been beaten 18-0 by Munster in the RDS that same weekend.

It was pretty grim for me, walking up to Paulie and shaking his hand and smiling for the waiting media. All the talk was about Munster that morning. They were reigning Heineken Cup champions. Leinster were reigning Magners League champions but, me?

I felt like a bit of a loser that morning as I stood for the photo-call with the Munster captain.

Twelve months later, all had changed.

We were Heineken Cup champs and we had just beaten them 30-0 in the RDS, less than 48 hours earlier. I'm not sure what was in Paulie's head as we stood in St Stephen's Green and smiled and gave our serious stares into the cameras and chatted to the media that morning.

I like Paulie.

He's a sound bloke.

Weirdly, he and I are also Evertonians – supporters of Everton football club since we were both just out of high infants. I have great respect for him and as a captain he is clever and genuine in his role with Munster.

On the morning of Monday, October 4, 2010, Paulie and I were back at it with Rory Best for another Heineken Cup launch, this time in the beautifully built Grand Canal Theatre in Dublin. Neither Paulie nor I had played in Leinster's 13-9 win a couple of days earlier. We were both eagerly looking forward to getting back into action and, with Paulie still struggling with his long-term groin problem, I was going to beat him to it.

But was I really Leinster captain that morning? I was still not so sure in my own head. As I stood there with Paulie, I wondered what was really in Joe Schmidt's head. I wanted to know. While I was standing there representing Leinster to the rest of Europe, I was actually bursting to find out where I really stood within the Leinster camp.

Moss Keane died that same week.

And, an era in Irish rugby died with him. I'd seen Moss play in lots of old video footage, and I'd had the honour of meeting the man on several occasions. It was hard not to notice him, the width of the man alone.

Whenever I looked at old photographs of Irish teams from the '70s, you'd see all sorts of body shapes amongst the forwards and, while Willie John McBride was a big man, when Moss was standing in the back row there always seemed to be so much more of him. All the guys on either side of him resembled bean poles.

With rugby becoming more and more a game of genetics, imagine if Moss as a young man had been placed on a proper fitness and strengthening programme. As he was, he was 100 per cent natural, nothing artificial, and he was still on a different physical level to most other players in the Five Nations. His hands! His arms! Very few men in Ireland, in any sport, were like that. We see them in other countries, like South Africa and in the Pacific Islands, where guys are unnaturally huge, but we have never been blessed with those genes in Ireland.

Moss Keane was also a true character and men like that are in shorter supply in Irish rugby nowadays. With players going into academies and onto programmes at a very young age, it is easy for the great majority to become institutionalised. We still get a few lads with wilder streaks in them, and that is a good thing because it's important to have some balance in a dressing room.

Mal O'Kelly may have been one of the last great characters in Leinster and Irish rugby. He always had his own way of doing things and, in addition to that, he was unbelievably laid back 90 per cent of the week. I'd watch him and wonder. When it mattered, all of a sudden he'd have an amazingly single-minded focus on what he was doing. Like in games – the tougher the opposition, the better Mal would always be.

He was thirty-six years old when he retired as a Leinster player, and I actually think he went too soon. He was in great shape, even then. He was a great man to be around. He mixed with everyone – again, just like Moss – but, I don't believe Moss spent as much of his life on distant planets as Mal O'Kelly did. The big quote from Mal's lips, which will out-live him, and remains in the air in the Leinster camp forever, was a statement he made several years before he retired.

"What's the point in having a schedule?" he asked the team's assembled coaches one afternoon, raising the paper in his hand into the air, and highly indignant that everyone in the room appeared to be working to completely different timelines than what he was reading.

"WHAT'S THE POINT?" asked Mal, a second time, whereupon the player next to him took the piece of paper out of Mal's hand and examined it.

"That's last week's schedule, Mal."

At the ERC launch in the Grand Canal Theatre on the Monday morning, all the big talk had been about Pool Two being a real-life 'Group of Death', and it did look especially nasty to me. Clermont, Saracens, and Racing Metro: the reigning French champions, the runners-up in the English Premiership, and Racing (one of the teams in Europe with a bagfull of household names and a budget which was still bursting at the seams). Obviously, I took advantage of that and told all the journalists that anyone could win the group.

The other pools?

They were all tricky, especially Pool One with Edinburgh, Castres, Northampton and Cardiff. No top-tier teams in there, I thought, but you'd never guess who might win through. Cardiff wear teams down and teams have to be up for it, physically, against them because they have such big ball carriers. They've got the Kiwi influence (in Rush, Tito and Laulala), and then they'd got Paterson and Parks, which made them dangerous. I thought Cardiff would win the group.

Edinburgh, I guessed, would be as hard to beat at home as they always have been, but they'd win no points away. Castres, equally, had a strong home record, and we'd experienced that 'treat' when we lost to them in 2009. And Northampton? They're a team on the way up in England, and they got through their pool the previous season, but their potential was balanced out by inexperience, in my opinion. But, with a solid coaching structure, and a good head on the team, I expected them to make it competitive for Cardiff.

Pool Three was Munster's to win. Toulon had Thomond Park on their schedule early, and since they 'don't travel', it was easy to see Munster 'managing' their way to the knockout stages in a typically efficient manner. Ospreys are serious opposition at any time, as we found out in the 2010 Magners League final, and London-Irish can cause problems with their blitz defence. Munster just needed a few points on the road to top the group.

Biarritz looked favourites in Pool Four. They looked good to win all their home games and get bonus points, plus get full points from Aironi away. Also, it was hard to see the French lose by more than seven points to Bath and Ulster. Bath have a strong future but they are too up and down with their performances. If Ulster got over Biarritz in Ravenhill then I thought they would be in the hunt as well.

Leicester looked certain to win Pool Five, winning all of their home games and beating Scarlets and Treviso away. Perpignan had a right to target all three games at home, but they were sure to struggle on the road to Scarlets and Tigers. Scarlets didn't have the consistency. I just saw one team, Leicester.

And one team in Pool Six, Toulouse.

They had Wasps, who are on a downward slide, Glasgow, who don't have the budget to compete as seriously as they would wish, and the Dragons, who'd be doing well for themselves to have beaten Glasgow and Wasps.

Clermont were strong favourites with the bookmakers to win our group, but that didn't worry me. It's all about managing yourself and holding onto control of your own destiny in the Heineken Cup! That's what Munster have taught everyone else in Europe for well over a decade.

The big question for everyone every year was, who are you going to beat away from home? And, where are you going to pick up a bonus point or two? We needed to win our three home games and try to pick up a few bonus points. If we lost two away games and won the other one, then we'd be pretty much where we needed to be at the end of the pool games.

Every team has to be realistic about its prospects and then has to 'manage' its way through six games. We knew it would be tough having Racing Metro first up. We did not know too much about them and, therefore, it would have been easy to take them a little lightly on home territory.

When the time came and they ran onto the field at the RDS, I could not believe the size of them. With Joe, we had already got into the routine of putting up posters of all the opposing players on the walls in our training camp in Riverview, with all of their details underneath each photo, and with five strengths and five weaknesses added for good measure to each individual. We knew Racing were going to be big but they were an unbelievable size, easily the biggest club side I have ever seen playing in Europe.

They were like a bunch of grizzly bears, I thought, as I stood on the sideline. It was also amusing to watch them before the game.

Their owner, the wealthy Parisian property tycoon Jacky Lorenzetti, was there, standing on the sideline, too, in his scarf and Racing Metro jacket and, incredibly, every single Racing player shook hands with the man as they ran out by him onto the field. Some even stooped down to add a kiss on the cheek!

The lads had mentioned to me during the week before the game that Sebastien Chabal was now thought to be paid €1million per year with Racing, making him the highest paid rugby player in the world. I didn't know if that was complete rubbish or not. But lots of teams have money at different times available to them, and some spend it wisely and some spend it loosely. It will not be known for a few years whether some of the French teams, like Racing and Toulon, have invested their money wisely or not. Whereas, you look at Toulouse down in the south of the country, steeped in tradition and fully knowledgable about how to perform and win. Rugby has never had a situation before where some teams, like Chelsea and Manchester City in football in England, have decided to buy their way to the very top.

I'd played against Chabal a few times, when he was a Sale player. He's a formidable athlete, with amazing strength and power and he's 'proper, proper' strong! When he is on the front foot, it is very hard to stop him. He makes the big hits and he also likes to do some flashy items on the side. However, if Chabal gets hit a couple of times pretty hard, he does not have too much of an appetite for more of the same. He's only human, and if any human being keeps getting massive hits full-on, then it takes a super-human character within that person to keep on looking for the ball.

They were all under pressure, with or without Mr Lorenzetti looking at them up close! They had picked a full-strength squad, and they had come to Dublin to do a job on us. Clear as day. Coming off the high of defeating Munster in the magnificent Aviva stadium in front of a huge crowd, I worried before the game began that we might be caught unawares. The most dangerous games in the group for us were the back-to-back games against Clermont in December. They thought they should have beaten us in the quarter-final in 2009-10 and, after that game, they had no fear of us. Talk about strong ball carriers! And since we'd met them in the quarter-final in the RDS, they had signed on the Kiwi, Sione Lauaki who is as strong as they come. If you don't believe me, just watch the clip of him on YouTube handing off Richie McCaw.

First time I saw the group, I thought... *Oh, no!*

At the same time, we knew that we had not been at our best against Clermont that same night in the RDS, and we were completely off our game at times. At home this season, they'd already blitzed most teams, and so we knew it was imperative for us to get something out of our trip to their home town. Clermont back-to-back was pivotal. It was good to have them away first. I always like that. It is harder to beat someone at home and then turn up in their place and beat them again. It's purely the psychology of it but, if you lose to someone away, then it is always easier to mentally step up a level a week later when you have them at home.

That's how it works in my head, anyhow.

But, there was potential trouble in Pool Two wherever we looked – like Saracens, who'd built serious momentum under Brendan Venter. He'd given them real belief.

My thoughts were: we beat Racing first of all, then they lose again and, by the time we play them a second time in the final game in the pool in Paris, they may have lost interest in the whole thing. Simple plan.

The weekend before we met them in the RDS, I'd watched them lose 28-23 to Toulouse on my TV, but they gained a bonus point and ended the night as Top 14 leaders. They were dogged against Toulouse, and the game forcibly reminded me just how attrittional French rugby has become. They really piled into one another from the very first minute.

The Monday morning after defeating Munster had been the happiest Monday morning we'd had since Joe's arrival. Heads were up. There was no buzz, because everyone knew we'd just won a League game, but there was a heightened sense of expectation. Supporters and journalists get quite excited about games between Munster and ourselves but, to us, it's just another game, and it has been a long time since anyone in our camp has considered these games as being extra-personal.

However, the game had left a cloud of dust and controversy in the air, after Lifeimi Mafi was banned for seven weeks for a tackle on Gordon D'Arcy. It was a high price for him and Munster to pay. Mafi is a seriously talented player, but it was a 'borderline' tackle.

It was a crucial moment, because it was a scoring opportunity for us and it did not get picked up by the officials. I should admit to going fairly nuts in the box, alongside Joe and Jono, when it happened. Later on, Mafi actually got a yellow card for a tackle on Rob Kearney, which did not have much to it at all.

Darce didn't complain too much. He never does. He is so solidly put together that he can take huge punishment without slowing down or looking for any sympathy whatsoever. He manages himself brilliantly and people forget that, in most games nowadays in Europe, he is coming up against players who might be 15 or 20 kilos heavier than him. Darce is so low to the ground and so dynamic, his change of pace is mesmerising, as is his footwork in a confined area. While Drico is more aggressive and more explosive, Darce has the more exceptional feet.

As the days counted down to the arrival of Racing Metro on the Saturday, our forwards worked hard preparing to dismantle their drive. The drive is such a fundemental part of the Racing game. They do not play flashy rugby. Instead, they prefer to run over the top of teams, and, in their mindset, our pack needed to be right up for that challenge.

As for me?

I needed to step back midweek.

That's how it is in the professional game. If you are not in the match 23, then, in truth, you are going to get in the way.

It was hard for me to take that physical, and mental, step back from the team as the first Heineken Cup game came into view. But we had Jonny back and that was a huge boost to everybody. He had come off the bench and saw us home against Munster and he always brings such confidence to the dressing room. That is no slight on Shaun Berne, who had stepped in for Jonny when he was injured a year earlier and acquitted himself extremely well, but Jonny Sexton is such a key player in the Leinster team.

I was edgy.

On the Friday night at home, I'd nothing to do.

In the warm-up at the RDS, I found it hard to take my eyes off Frans Steyn. The South African can drop goals with relative ease from 50 metres and, as I stood on the sideline, I could only marvel as he knocked the ball over and over again from 65 metres or so. The ball was like a torpedo leaving his boot. Actually, it was frightening watching him.

My job was to run water for the team during the game which, to be honest, is always fine by me, even if it is a slightly weird experience. You are on the field with the water but, at the same time, you are completely helpless. But, given a choice between running water or sitting in the stand, I'd put my hand up for 'water boy' duty any time! At least you can burn up some energy during the course of the evening.

Our front row was, more or less, a whole new unit for the first game of the Heineken Cup campaign, and it remained to be seen how they would fare against Andrea Lo Cicero, Benjamin Noirot and Juan Pablo Orlandi. We had confidence in the lads and Richardt Strauss had done really well against Munster, but he remained an 'unknown quantity' at Heineken Cup level. With Stan Wright out injured, Mike Ross was also stepping up and taking his opportunity for the first time, with both hands, as a Leinster player. With Dev Toner and Hinesy in the second row, it was a big change from the Leinster front five which had helped bring home the Heineken Cup less than two years earlier.

However, Racing were also holding their breath before the game. They had a big decision to make at out-half, where Hernandez and Wisniewski were both injured, and their coach, Pierre Berbizier, had their regular scrum-half, Jerome Fillol, moving over to No. 10 with Nicolas Durand starting alongside him.

Just over one minute into the game, Chabal formally introduced himself to Jamie and left him flat on his back. That's Chabal for you, he can be a real physical threat, with or without the ball, and if he catches any player even slightly off balance then there's going to be trouble. Jamie was run-over.

But Chabal's moment of glory didn't linger for too long. We kicked long, they regained possession, and Chabal came charging again – and, this time, the resulting tackle had a bigger impact on the game than any tackle prior to that or any tackle for the remainder of the game. You see, Isa had Chabal in his sights.

If I had to pick one man on our whole team, from the entire collection of backs and forwards, to do a proper job in the tackle on Sebastien Chabal then it would be Isa Nacewa.

He hits harder for his weight than any other player in the Leinster squad, and he hits hard consistently. He's a freak like that. In so many other ways on the field he is one of the most talented players I have ever seen, but, in the tackle, he always amazes me.

Chabal had the ball well tucked.

Everyone in the ground had their eyes glued to him.

Whack!

Isa thumped into him and the RDS went nuts. It was also like a bolt of energy hit every single Leinster player on the field. That tackle quietened Chabal down somewhat, and then on his next big carry he was met by Dev and Hinesy. After that Mike Ross put in a great tackle on Vulivuli. Seeing Mike doing that, lifted everyone in a blue jersey even more. They had their massive pack, but we had them under control. We had one scrum turnover on the board early enough. We were also knocking them back all over the field. Our ball in the air was also excellent.

Ball in the air was one of Joe's number one priorities from day one. He wanted us to dominate the space in the air, always. And, we did that against Racing, with Rob Kearney and Isa winning every time.

By the end of the evening, our entire game had come together very well and all of the hard work by Joe and the coaching team could be seen in the team display. We had some great running lines and our off-loading was top quality. We'd also scored five tries by the end of the night's work, which was a fantastic return for Jamie and the lads.

There was also a downside, there always is, and our discipline at the ruck was not brilliant, and referee Dave Pearson punished us too often for not rolling away in the tackle. Also, Drico damaged his hamstring when he turned quickly and tried to chase down Vulivuli, and that left doubts over him for three or four weeks. It also has to be said that, in the first 20 minutes of the game, we were slow to take command on the field.

We were only 6-3 in front after 27 minutes. With Jonny still resting his kicking leg, Isa had knocked over two penalties and Fillol had replied with one for them. Then two tries in the space of five minutes gave us the daylight we wanted, with Seanie and Kearns crossing Racing's line.

Seanie's came off a good break. Straussy ran a great line, Darce showed brilliant feet, and Seanie and Mike carried the ball to a couple of metres from their line. From the resulting ruck, Seanie powered over. The second try was the result of some Drico and Jonny combined magic and, after Jonny looped around, Kearns was in! That second try was, I'll admit, poetic to watch. All too often, even those of us who are Drico's team-mates for years have to stand back and wonder how he actually makes things happen on the field. The number of defenders he took out. The space he left.

Unbelievable, simply unbelievable!

We consolidated our position on the field very quickly in the second half, which was so important, and Straussy was soon over for a try. Jamie and Fergus McFadden got our fourth and fifth tries. Ferg must have run his in from all of 60 metres, before touching down in the corner.

The tries were great to watch. I enjoyed all five of them, but we gave away so many penalties, and one of them Steyn must have hit from 70 metres. Vulivuli also scored a try for them when he steamrolled over three or four people and, midway through the second half, we were only seven points in front, 26-19, when we should really have been out of sight. At that time, the game was actually in the balance and we only had ourselves to blame.

We were never going to give the perfect performance against Racing. Five tries in a big scoring win and a bonus point in the bag left everyone more than happy, and there was nobody happier than our doc, Professor Arthur Tanner.

Arthur is such an important and calming figure in the background for the Leinster team and he has been a rock of comfort for all of us for many years. He's also our good friend.

But, on Monday, as we watched snatches of the Racing game on video and Ferg was blistering up the touchline for his try, we all saw someone we knew very well dancing a little jig in front of the main RDS stand.

I had to look a second time…

It was Arthur alright! I think he was giving it the cowboy dance by pretending to shoot two handguns into the air.

I spent the weekend, as I tend to do, especially on Heineken Cup weekends, watching every single game on television from Friday through to Sunday, either live or recorded. And I thought Saracens made a great battle of their visit to Stade Marcel Michelin in Clermont. They lost 25-10 in the end, and were very unlucky to be denied a bonus point. If anything, Sarries should have taken even more from the game because Clermont played poorly enough. Sarries out-half, Derick Hougaard, missed a penalty from in front of the posts (he only kicked two from five, all told) and their full-back, Alex Goode, dropped the ball over the line after a slashing break.

By the end of the weekend we had five points and Clermont had four points and, even with only one round of games played, that was a massive position to find ourselves in because bonus points were sure to be so precious and difficult to pick up in Pool Two.

I watched Munster lose to London-Irish live on my television and 'Irish' blew them away in the first 60 minutes. Munster got their bonus point at the very end and that looked to be so important for them. Toulon won late over Ospreys. I still backed Munster to do what had to be done to get out of that pool, but it was clear already that it was going to be a tight call.

In the tightest 'call' of all on the opening weekend, Alex Tuilagi went over for a last-ditch try to save Leicester from an amazing defeat in Treviso. It was 34-29 in the end. It was incredible stuff. I kept recording everything! Equally incredible was Toulouse just getting by Wasps at home, 18-16. But one of the most enjoyable games of the weekend was Scarlets beating Perpignan 43-34, despite losing 5-4 to the French on the try count.

The Heineken Cup was up and running alright.

Heineken Cup
Pool Two
RDS, Dublin
October 9, 2010

Leinster 38, Racing Metro 22

HT: Leinster 21, Racing Metro 6
Attendance: 17,936
Man of the Match: Sean O'Brien
Referee: Dave Pearson (England)

—⚹—

Scoring sequence – **5 Mins:** Nacewa pen 3-0; 12: Fillol pen 3-3; **27:** Nacewa pen 6-3; **30:** O'Brien try, Nacewa con 13-3; **35:** Kearney try 18-3; **37:** Steyn pen 18-6; **39:** Nacewa pen 21-6. **Half time 21-6;** 41: Fillol pen 21-9; **48:** Strauss try 26-9; **51:** Steyn pen 26-12; **57:** Vulivuli try, Fillol con 26-19; **65:** Heaslip try, Nacewa con 33-19; **68:** Fillol pen 33-22; **79:** McFadden try 38-22.

Leinster: R Kearney; I Nacewa, B O'Driscoll (F McFadden 57), G D'Arcy, L Fitzgerald; J Sexton (S Horgan 74), E Reddan (I Boss 59); H van der Merwe (C Healy 52), R Strauss (J Harris-Wright 74), M Ross (S Shawe 72); N Hines, D Toner; S O'Brien, S Jennings (D Ryan 67), J Heaslip, Capt.

Racing Metro: F Steyn; S Bobo, A Vulivuli, A Masi (M Bergamasco 52), J Saubade; J Fillol, N Durand (M Loree 66); A Lo Cicero (J Brugnaut 73), B Noirot (C Festuccia 58), JP Orlandi (S Zimmerman 78); L Nallet, Capt., J Qovu Nailiko (S Dellape 58); J Leo'o (R Vaquiin 78), J Cronje, S Chabal (A Battut 52).

CHAPTER TWO

"GOOD... YOU'LL BE ON THE BENCH."

Joe Schmidt

Amongst other things, my family were farmers.

My mother, Paula, grew up in Dublin but was always passionate about animals, particularly horses. Frank, my dad, had farming and butchering in his family background, even though he largely swapped that lifestyle for the more corporate world of business in Dublin.

As Frank spent his working week in the city, it was soon left to Mum to look after the farm and, as I like to remind her, she therefore became the 'slave driver' in our family home. In truth, Mum instilled a strong work ethic in every member of our family.

There was my sister, Sarah, who was two years older than me, and my younger brother, Owen, who was five years behind me. I spent a number of years in the Wicklow Montessori School, but from the age of eight things changed. After that, every morning at 7.30am we would load up into the back of Dad's car and head off on our 20-mile trip to school in Dublin. For me, that was first to Willow Park, before I progressed to Blackrock College. Owen followed the same path.

Along the way, we also dropped Sarah to Killiney where she was attending The Holy Child. The return journey home was never so simple, however.

Some days, we would get the Dart to Bray, followed by the old diesel train to Greystones, and that would, in turn, be followed by the 84 bus to Newcastle. Nevertheless, it was always a great little adventure for the three of us.

On the days on which I had rugby after school, I would sometimes get the bus into the city centre where Dad was working, and I'd get a lift home late with him. All in all, I think these experiences left all three of us feeling pretty independent.

My dad had built our family home, before I was born, just up the road from where he himself had been reared, at Coyne's Cross between

37

Newtownmountkennedy and Ashford. Mum always had horses and ponies at the house and, as time moved on, Dad bought some more land, which had been in the Cullen family for over 200 years, from one of his brothers. The farm itself was up in the hills behind Newtownmountkennedy at the end of an old, narrow road, which was more of a lane, and must have been all of a mile and a half long. It was at this stage that my family also got into cattle, and sheep, too. My parents subsequently built again at the start of this lane, and this is where the family now lives.

I have to say I had a brilliant childhood, growing up with Sarah looking after me and me looking after Owen! My mum ensured that we all worked hard, whether that was on the farm or, at times, with my uncle, Liam, who had a butcher's shop in Wicklow town – or even the odd trip to the abbatoir where the animals were taken from the farm and killed every Monday.

As a young Wicklow boy, I had nothing at my fingertips except space. Nothing! All my school friends were living in the city, and there weren't too many lads my own age around the place looking to kick a ball around, or take up a rugby ball and run with it in the large back garden behind our house, where I'd spend hours and hours every single day playing fifteen-man games of rugby all on my own. Usually, I'd be filling all fifteen Irish shirts. And the garden was Lansdowne Road.

The trees on one side were one touchline, while the other touchline was the paved area on the opposite side. At one end of the garden there was a gate into a paddock. This was the opposition goalposts, New Zealand's or England's most often, and after deciding who was going to score what try for Ireland, and in what order, I'd line up the conversions in the direction of that gate.

The gate at the other end was, it so happened, awkwardly situated in the corner of the garden, leading into a large field. The opposition kicked their penalties and conversions into this more difficult end of Lansdowne Road.

Occasionally, after watching Meath play Dublin in Croke Park, the garden would change to Croker, but most days it stayed as Lansdowne Road.

Ireland wouldn't beat New Zealand all of the time.

There were some gallant defeats, when Ireland were 20 points down and just ran out of time for a famous victory but, two days out of every three,

Ireland walked off the field in triumph. I'd also walk off shagged tired, because playing in fifteen positions on a rugby team for 80 minutes is no easy feat.

I was lucky in that, no matter what sporting event was on, I could turn the garden or one of the fields beside the house into a great sporting arena. Everton had some great victories there! When Wimbledon was on, I would have a tennis court up against the garage wall. Come the Ryder Cup or one of the majors, I had a great golf course laid out in front of me.

During my two years living in Leicester, Shane Jennings and I had fallen – hook, line and sinker – for the TV programme, Grand Designs, which has its host, Kevin McCloud, visiting people all over Britain and Ireland who are in the throes of building their own homes, and when I came back to live in Ireland, in 2007, I immediately started into my own build.

But, within 12 months, the worst recession we have ever known hit the country. I continued building, even though Mr McCloud never did visit me!

I was happy with the result of my own grand design.

When I finally made my decision to play again, I just wanted to get back into the thick of the action immediately. It had been five and a half months since the surgery on my left shoulder. I had decided to make myself available for team selection sooner than my consultant, Len Funk, would have wished. But, I wanted to do it.

I thought that Joe would want me to start against Saracens at Wembley in our second Heineken Cup group game. I popped into his office at Riverview to tell him that I was good to go.

"Good... You'll be on the bench." Joe replied, instantly.

I wanted to start against Sarries. I wanted to be on the starting 15, and I wanted to see how long I could last out there.

But, Joe saw it differently.

He'd already made it clear in the opening few months of his time in Leinster that he didn't give a damn about reputations. He picked guys who were playing well, first and foremost, and he had seen Dev Toner and Hinesy do a great job in the second row against Munster in the Aviva, and also against Racing Metro in our first Heineken Cup group game.

Everyone in the camp had been looking forward to getting to Wembley and playing there. It was a real once-in-a-lifetime opportunity.

I had been looking forward to it as well.

Drico was ruled out of the chance of playing at Wembley because of his pulled hamstring. He had to make his appearance on perhaps the most famous stretch of grass in world sport as a 'water boy', taking over those duties from me. At least he knew he'd get to run across the grass.

I was on the bench.

I was also nervous. I wasn't at all sure if I had made the right decision in coming back so soon.

At the same time, I still wished I was starting the game. It would have been easier for me to start the game rather than sit on the bench. That way, you are into things straightaway. Your mind does not have enough time to dwell on any doubts, and there were so many doubts in my head.

We flew over to London on the Friday afternoon and had a bit of a run out in the ground, even though the Wembley officials were not delighted to see us heading out there. They didn't want us doing anything at all out on their field.

Sarries had their own agreement with the groundsmen and, each time they did their Captain's Run, they reduced it to a walk-through instead.

But, Joe wanted to do more than that. He got some defensive drills up and running and, by the end of the afternoon, the groundsmen were very unhappy with their Irish visitors.

We knew that Saracens would be fighting for their lives in their first home game. They'd played very expansively in their 25-10 defeat in Clermont a week earlier, and they'd taken confidence from that, no doubt.

They were expecting 45,000 people to show up in Wembley, which had become their 'home from home' in the 2009-10 season when they had four wins from four games, defeating the touring South Africans, as well as Northampton, Worcester and Harlequins.

Brendan Venter, their Director of Rugby, also had them thinking like winners. Venter, who's also a medical practitioner in Cape Town, is larger than life and, whatever else, he had made a big impression in Saracens in a short space of time.

Venter talks about the guys in his dressing room improving as people, as well as rugby players. He's into some fairly serious head stuff and he didn't mind telling the British rugby press that he'd got his players to write him an essay about being 'the ideal twenty-year-old'. He wanted his players to tell him what the twenty-year-old would look like, how he'd treat alcohol, how he'd treat women, how he'd handle his finances.

He does it his way, but it seemed to work for Brendan in England straightaway, because Saracens had been undefeated at home for almost twelve months, and, in his first season, they'd only just lost a thrilling Premiership final to Leicester at the end of the season. He was a winner as a player and came on in the famous World Cup final victory over New Zealand in 1995. But, he's also pretty forthright in expressing his views and he had a fourteen-week ban for misconduct handed down in his first year with Sarries as well.

Joe had done massive analysis of all the Sarries players, as usual, and it helped that he could make a few phone calls to Clermont. He was told that the lads there were nursing more bumps and bruises than they'd felt for some time after their contest with Sarries a week earlier.

We knew a lot about them.

We knew, also, that Steve Borthwick would have picked apart our lineout. He runs a pretty good show, to be fair, and I suppose he is a bit like me when all is said and done – he's simply a lineout nerd!

Sarries also have a very set way in which they play and, mostly, they like to hit the middle as often as possible. Their props and second rows crash things up the middle. We were prepared for that.

Sarries are one of the wealthy clubs in the English game. They are certainly an ambitious club and, really, they are strong throughout the field: Their scrum, lineout, and kicking game, are all fairly rock solid.

At the end of the game, Sarries went through 30 phases and they had us backed up against a wall, but they didn't break us down, and their season took an early nose-dive with their narrow loss to us. It was 25-23. Hectic stuff. But we defended calmly all the same and I got the impression that we could have defended all day against them if we had to do so.

I was on the field with 11 minutes to go.

And, first thing I did was give away a penalty which brought them to within those two points of us.

The scoreline had been 25-20 when I went in. I gave away the penalty for not rolling away at the tackle. I also missed a tackle on Schalk Brits. I'd pushed up on the short side and he cut back inside me. He had really fast feet.

I felt sluggish.

I really struggled to get into the game in those 11 minutes. And, after giving away the penalty, I became completely paranoid about giving away a second.

I was also very apprehensive, waiting for my first tackle, wondering how it would feel on my shoulder. When I got out there I wasn't swinging into tackles. I wasn't at all instinctive. A large part of me was holding back. I knew it wouldn't have been like that if I'd started the game.

Joe had told me, before going in, to doubly warn the guys not to give away any penalties. So, the minute I was on the field, the only thought in my head was, *Don't give away a penalty!*

As usual, when you drill it into your brain not to do something, that's exactly what you end up doing. Like when you are playing golf and issue yourself an instruction... "Don't drive into the water!"

And you drive into the water!

I was thinking, *No penalties!*

And what did I do?

And what was I afraid of doing for the remainder of the game?

I had a few testers on my shoulder, but nothing huge. I actually didn't touch the ball once in those 11 minutes, but I got through it, made a few decent tackles I thought and, all in all, while it was not the most memorable 11 minutes of my professional rugby career, it gave me back some of my confidence.

If I'd been a younger player, still getting to grips with the ins and outs of my career, then I might have been on the verge of some crisis of confidence. When you are thrown into a high pressure environment and you don't feel exactly right, your head swimming with uncertainties and some doubt, it's easy to have a bit of a meltdown.

After the game, Jamie had one thing to say to me.

"One hundred per cent!" he said, laughing, as he walked by me in the dressing room. "Still one hundred per cent!"

He hadn't lost a game as Leinster captain, and he took full enjoyment from reminding me of that important fact.

He had led the team brilliantly at Wembley. We had started quite slowly, but we settled down and got into our stride before and after half time. No doubt about it, Jamie did a really good job. But, on the morning of the game, I had struggled to get a handle on the mood of the squad in the team hotel.

Too many of the players were a bit giddy, I thought.

However, I also had to remind myself that the team was changing, that it was evolving, and more and more younger guys with a different outlook on preparation were coming into the match squad.

Jonny, of course, is incredibly influential. Fergus McFadden is coming through. Rob Kearney has been central to everything for a while now. These lads, and the other young players, all tend to be quite relaxed on the day of a game, and much more so than I am.

Some of the younger lads like to mess about quite a bit, and that is no bad thing sometimes. Everyone prepares differently. It's good that they can be relaxed, because I know for sure that when they go out onto the field they are always ready for the battle.

My first thought, after walking into the dressing room at one of the most famous grounds in the whole world of sport, was that this place is not a patch on the Aviva. Naturally, dressing rooms for soccer teams tend to be on the smaller side, but there were no plunge pools like we now have in the Aviva, and the television screens were on the small side as well. In the

Aviva, there are huge flat screens on the walls of the dressing rooms which make the place look really cool and state-of-the-art.

My role in there, before the game, was to be as supportive as I could be and, at the same time, I had to get my head right for when I was coming into the game.

I thought I'd have come on earlier in the game.

On the sideline, I was getting really antsy. Naturally, you think that when the clock hits the 60-minute mark that you are sure to be going on. Then, it goes by the 60 minutes. Suddenly, it's 65 minutes, 66 minutes. With the clock counting down, the danger is that you start to switch off slightly in your own head.

All week I was waiting to find out how my shoulder would be when I got into the game. I wanted to find out what would happen. What would the first hit feel like?

After waiting five and a half months, every single minute on the sideline was like a full 10 minutes. Waiting. Wondering and guessing. How did my shoulder reconstruction really go?

Every year I've wondered to myself, will I be able to get through another year of rugby? But, sitting on the sideline at Wembley, I was left wondering if I could get through another game.

Drico did what he had to do, handing out the water and doing it as seriously and efficiently as any 'water boy' in the history of the Leinster rugby team.

He is enjoying playing with Leinster more than he has ever done in his life, that much is clear, every single day. And, he's such a competitor. All the time. In the dressing room. Out on the training field. When he is training he is perhaps the most competitive person we have.

Very few professional rugby players have that competitive instinct. At training, I spend a great deal of my time thinking about the next game, and what we need to be doing in order to ensure that we win that game.

Sarries' 30 phases in the final minutes of the game made for the required drama at the end alright. But, in truth, they lacked the experience they needed to close the game out. We knew exactly what they would do, and they didn't let us down.

Apart from a brief period in the first half, they never looked like they could stretch us. Alex Goode scored their try after 12 minutes, which came off a lineout drive, and strong carries subsequently by Mouritz Botha and Andy Saull. They led 8-3, but they were never able to lift their game to a higher level.

Even when Straussy was sin-binned in the 61st minute, Sarries stuck to 'Plan A' and that suited us just fine. Afterwards, Venter went off on one. He said the referee should have had two more of us in the bin and that Monsieur Berdos should have hit us with another 50 penalty decisions!

It was rash, but not surprising talk from their coach. In actual fact, I felt Straussy was unlucky to have to go. He's just such a total rugby player, and with his experience as a flanker in his home country he offers so much to the team, all over the field. In his first year with Leinster he got very few opportunities, mainly because he had two such seasoned professionals, in Bernard Jackman and John Fogarty, standing in his way, but I'd watched him playing some games for Blackrock and he looked to be made of the right stuff.

Brendan Venter's comments came across as sour grapes to me. He claimed that they had played all of the rugby. He obviously thought that the way they'd played was attractive to watch but, that's not the way I saw it.

Monsieur Berdos, I thought, was very tough on us. Of course, we gave away too many penalties during the game, and that was what started the Sarries' coach off on his rant. The exact penalty count was 16-8 in their favour, and the referee gave them eight penalties to just two for us in the second half and, by the end of the game, it was pretty obvious to me that he was only refereeing one side.

The Heineken Cup is refereed very differently to the Premiership in England, and some of the English clubs complain as a result. In the Premiership, they roll away very quickly, while in the Six Nations and in Europe there is more contact at the breakdown. It's more 'hands away' in the Premiership and they never contest the breakdown quite as hard.

I thought that the referee was harsh on me when I gave away the penalty, for instance, because he felt I did not get out of the way quickly enough. In reality, he was giving no time for play to unfold. However, hand on heart, I've always found so many of these decisions to be 50-50 and it's best for a team to work with whatever referee they have on a particular day. Just like players, referees are programmed at times and, on occasions during games, they often start refereeing only one of the teams on the field. It's human nature for referees to fall in with the team which appears to be playing all the rugby. This was partly our own fault, too, because once more after doing so much excellent work early on in the game we had dropped off and stopped taking the game to Sarries. We invited them on.

Both Sarries and Mr Berdos.

Once we kept our shape defensively, we had no real trouble containing them and it was only when they put the ball into the wider channels that things looked dangerous for us, because they had good pace and footwork out there. They got soft yards for a couple of phases. We had to be so strict with ourselves to keep rolling away. We couldn't contest the breakdown like we would have wanted, so, in effect, we let them have the ball, and that's how they went through their phases at the very end. Eventually, they knocked it on. Game over. We had our away win and a vital nine points in the pool.

Sexto kicked seven from seven, which was another brilliant display. His try, in the 52nd minute, which he converted to push us 22-11 in front, was one of our best tries of the season. It was after that that Monsieur Berdos suddenly had us in his sights and began to give penalty after penalty award against us, including sending Straussy off when it looked quite clear to me that he had stayed on his feet as the arriving player when contesting for the ball.

What a 'game-breaker' of a try it was from Sexto! Shaggy chased and won Eoin Reddan's box kick, and then Straussy brilliantly won the ball on the deck. The ball was moved across the line for Isa to hand off a tackle, and Ferg McFadden provided the link before Jonny went in. It was Leinster poetry in motion.

In the pack, it was not exactly poetic. But we did have storming performances from Jenno and Jamie and, of course, Seanie O'Brien! He was phenomenal with his ball carries and, just as we see so often on the training field, he was skittling guys out of the way. He has become such a physical force in such a short space of time. The work he does on the field, and off it. He goes into the gym and he just explodes! He's massive. He's so well put together and he's so aggressive when he has the ball. The greatest thing of all is that Seanie wants that ball all of the time as well.

With Seanie in the side, doing what he does with Jenno and Jamie, it allows Hinesy and myself to carry out our roles without distraction and to hit those rucks and get the work done. We just want to get the ball into Seanie's hands as often as possible, and in some games he might carry the ball over twenty times, which is phenomenal.

He has also hit his stride brilliantly, because of the coaching and direction he is receiving from Joe.

Joe wants players with the ball in their hands, and he gives guys the licence to play the ball from wherever. We see that in training. It's different to anything we did before and it is obvious to everyone in the dressing room that we are a team which can now score more tries than we ever dreamed of before.

A dream had also come true for Simon Shawe, who made his European debut against Racing Metro as a substitute, and he also came into the game at Wembley with four minutes remaining for Mike Ross. Simon had been playing for Ballymena before getting the call-up from Leinster, at thirty-two years of age. We were lucky to pick him up when Stan suddenly damaged his Achilles, and Mike damaged his calf. Shawsy is proof, if ever rugby players in Ireland needed proof, that you should never give up on your dreams. Midway through his career, he had been on a development contract with Ulster but nothing more ever materialised for him at that point. Seeing what it meant to him gave everyone in our squad a fantastic boost.

Wembley had a strange feel to it throughout the day. The ground actually had the feel of a big concert event, with a band and fireworks and the most ridiculously annoying tune I have ever heard at a rugby game, which they insisted on playing over and over.

It's called, 'Stand Up for the Saracens', and it was written for the club by the band, Right Said Fred. It was so bad I had to purposely shake it out of my head as quickly as possible after the game. Still, in terms of real volume, the ground was not quite as electric as I had imagined Wembley would be (ever since watching Spurs beat Coventry in the first FA Cup final I can remember in the old ground!)

It was a good weekend for us, and for Munster who slammed Toulon 45-18 in typical Munster style. But Biarritz took a hold on Pool Four with a huge second-half performance over Ulster, for a 35-15 win and a bonus point.

Declan Kidney rang me the Monday after our victory over Sarries, to give me the bad news. He wasn't including me in his squad for the November Internationals, which was a bigger disappointment than I imagined it would be. It was just so frustrating. Paul O'Connell was out injured. I wanted games, now that I was back after my surgery, but there was nothing I could say to Deccie.

"Fair enough," I told him.

I thought he might pick me in the squad and then watch me against Connacht the following weekend in the Magners League, then make his decision. Instead, he wanted to go with Mick O'Driscoll and Donncha O'Callaghan, and have Dev on the bench.

"We're starting you this weekend," Joe told me, "but we're keeping Jamie as captain."

"Fine!" I said to Joe.

But, I was not feeling all that fine, in all honesty.

Joe, obviously, had watched Jamie lead the team and go 'three out of three' as team captain, so he was in no hurry to change things around now that he finally had the team winning games after such a slow, difficult start to the season.

Joe was making his decisions the way I wanted him to make his decisions but, it so happened, I didn't like the decision he made at the time. However, there was nothing to be gained from making a big deal of it or saying anything to Joe. It was not time for me to make an issue of anything. I had no option but to go out against Connacht and get my head right on the field, to play the sort of game I had been playing all of my life.

As it turned out, I struggled to get into the rhythm of the game in the first half at the Sportsground. We were playing up the hill and the whole team dogged its way along for the 40 minutes. We led 5-3 at half time, thanks to a try from Isa, after Isaac Boss blasted through a gap at the back of a lineout near the halfway line, and looped a pass out to the left. The second half went a little bit better for me.

We won 18-6.

It was always going to be a dogfight down there and that's how it turned out. I got into the flow of things in the second half because I'd been 'off' in contact situations up to then and, generally, just not getting into the game. Then, halfway through the second half, just as I felt I was getting somewhere, I was pulled off by Joe. Right on 60 minutes and right as we had planned before the game. Hinesy came in.

I was still disappointed.

All sorts of thoughts were going through my head while I was out there. I never felt more noticeable or more paranoid.

Everyone is watching me, I kept thinking.

Joe is watching me.

Deccie is watching me.

I then had to wait another long week for another game of rugby. We played Edinburgh the following Saturday, in the RDS.

Jamie was rested and Joe had me back in as team captain. I played a little bit better than I had against Connacht. We won 19-18 in a tight contest, which delighted Joe because it was five wins from five games in the month of October, which was a huge turnaround for him as a new coach in a new city. Andrew Conway got our try in the 46th minute. All that mattered to me was that we'd won and I'd played better.

Will I get a call now from Deccie? I was thinking, foolishly really, because the Irish coach could see as clearly as everyone else, that I was not yet right.

But I was captain.

I was feeling good about playing more aggressively.

I was happier.

Hey, I'd just played my first 80 minutes of rugby in over six months, why wouldn't I be feeling very happy?

There was no call from Deccie on the Monday morning.

I had gone to the Aviva to see Ireland against South Africa.

I was at a corporate lunch beforehand. It was a bit awkward, because you talk to so many people, and they all ask more or less the same questions, basically wondering why I was not in the Ireland squad.

It's hard not to feel a bit of a dud in those situations. But, you have to give a rosy picture, tell people how you've come back from injury and how everything is going just right and according to the great plan.

Ireland were not good against South Africa, and we were not much better against Samoa.

I decided to text Deccie.

'Hi Declan... Leo Cullen here! Making sure you haven't forgotten my number! Hope all's good!'

There was no text back from Deccie in reply.

That left me totally frustrated.

And completely freaked out that I'd done something stupid.

Mid-week, before Ireland played New Zealand, I got a call from Deccie who asked me to come in and train with the Irish squad. Finally. But it was a weird experience. I trained with Ireland in the morning and then trained with Leinster in the afternoon – because we were playing the Dragons that same weekend.

It was not an ideal schedule for me.

But, I needed to keep my head in the shop window. Somewhere in the shop window. It didn't matter where?

I went to the All Blacks game, once again as a fully-fledged Irish rugby supporter. I was still hoping to get another call from Deccie the following Monday but, as I took my seat, about eight or nine rows from the front, on the 22-metre line, I suddenly realised just how much I wanted to be out there.

It was cold and wet but there was a slightly greater buzz in the ground than there had been when Ireland played the Springboks.

During the game against the 'Boks, it didn't help that the people in front of me kept moving the whole damned time. They never stopped getting up and getting back into their seats. Everyone seemed just as worried about their next beer as they did about Ireland stopping the reigning world champions. Watching the game was a peculiar experience for me.

There was no atmosphere in the place and it was a disappointment to see a magnificent stadium like the Aviva failing to pass its first big test. It was a total let-down and, at the start of the second half, there must have been only 10,000 people in their seats.

Leinster kept on winning during the November Internationals, and we got four tries and a bonus point in our 27-6 win over the Dragons at the RDS. Shaggy got in for two tries and Shaun Berne got a try in his first start of the season, Bossy also crossed for a try.

The following Monday I was back in camp with Ireland. The lineout had not gone well against the Springboks or the All Blacks and I had thought that Deccie might give me a crack at it. All the same, it was not a bombshell when he told me he was sticking with the status quo.

But then he also told me that I needed to work on a few more things in my game, and I took that pretty hard. I felt really shitty after that conversation, but I had to train out the whole week with the Irish squad.

At the tail-end of November and the beginning of December, in the coldest weather any of us could ever remember on a rugby field, we lost to Ospreys and drew with Scarlets. Luckily, they had underground heating in both grounds and it was good to get both games out of the way and not have them thrown into the back end of the season. Games were cancelled almost everywhere else those two weekends.

They were not bad performances but there was a bit of panic gripping the squad, with too many injuries and too little time before the trip to Clermont, to Joe Schmidt's former home town. Andrew Conway scored his second senior try against the Ospreys and Isa also crossed in the second half, but we lost two men to the sin bin when Ed O'Donoghue and Ian Madigan both got yellow cards in the second half. It was 15-19 in the end. I'd played only okay, yet again, and I felt completely pissed off with myself, and with the season as it was unfolding in front of me.

A few days before we played the Scarlets, I felt my Achilles start to pinch. It had been niggling me for a long time, and it was taking me longer and longer to warm up in training. It was just that bit too tight. First thing in the morning, in my own home, it was also a pain in the backside, as I hobbled around for ten or fifteen minutes.

The sidelines in Llanelli, despite the underground heating, were pretty much like concrete. The rest of the field was crispy, but fine to play on. But, I could not get into my stride. Finally, I had to go off after 50 minutes, as I thought my Achilles was about to snap at any second.

I had plodded through the game up to that point, stuck in third gear. Hinesy came on for me. We were losing the game when I departed but the lads managed to get themselves together and salvaged a draw. Shaggy, Ferg McFadden and Eoin O'Malley scored our tries.

"How do you feel?" Joe asked me on the Monday morning after the Scarlets game. And I started talking to him, and couldn't stop myself.

Before I knew it, I realised that I was desperately trying to sell myself to him, and sell my case to start against Clermont in our third pool game in the Heineken Cup.

It was not how I had imagined my season unfolding.

"I know I haven't been playing great," I told Joe, "but if you are going to play me in either of the Clermont games, then play me in the away game."

I continued: "It will be tough out there ... it will suit me better."

And I then continued some more: "I'm totally up for it, Joe, the game will suit me out there in France."

In November I had been worried about not getting selected for Ireland but, suddenly, in December, the big worry for me was not getting picked for Leinster!

I felt so confused.

I wanted to be out there.

I felt the team needed me because we were short so many players, including Drico, Rob Kearney and Luke Fitzgerald. I knew I wasn't playing well, but I wanted to lead the team out against Clermont and prove to everyone watching me, and prove to myself, that I still had what Leinster needed. Ferg and Eoin O'Malley had come in and they had played with amazing confidence. They'd grabbed their opportunities.

For me, like a 'new boy' all over again myself, the buzz of Heineken Cup week was uplifting. Nobody felt we had a chance in Clermont.

Not a sniff.

It was really exciting.

Problem was, I didn't know for sure if I still had what Leinster needed. There were doubts in my mind presenting themselves as recurring obstacles. I knew I had to sit down for a long chat with Enda McNulty.

Enda is a former Armagh All-Ireland winning footballer, who is now a professional motivator for athletes and teams, and he had played a very important role within the Leinster team during the final years with Michael Cheika.

I loaded it all out on the table in front of Enda, including the difficulty of coming back from my shoulder surgery, my troublesome Achilles, the fact that I could not find any form, my low confidence levels, my utter confusion at times.

There was a lot to discuss.

Enda told me not to worry.

"What are you good at?" asked Enda, quite quickly.

He is brilliant at building up the positives within a player's career. I listed off all my strengths and abilities to him.

He spent most of our meeting reminding me of all the things I have done, and all the things I can still do, which other players cannot do.

That chat helped me enormously.

A few nights later, I watched a documentary on RTÉ which told the story of Jim Stynes in his courageous battle against an aggressive form of cancer. Stynes is a former Dublin Gaelic footballer and became one of the greatest players in the modern history of Australian Rules. A young man, in his early-40s, he was suddenly fighting for his life. His fight and especially his attitude and his massive bravery were inspirational.

Watching Jim Stynes fighting for his life made me sure that I could win my fight – after all, I was only fighting for my rugby career.

All my doubts and frustrations, and the total confusion which was overpowering me, were condensed at that point into one single problem. I needed to focus on my body.

The feeling that my body was quickly breaking down, and letting me down, had to be overcome. I was only a handful of games back after a serious piece of reconstructive surgery on my left shoulder, and what should I have expected? Enda McNulty told me to banish every, single negative thought in my head, and that's what I did.

"Your body is your business!" That is one of Enda's big phrases. And that phrase had become central to my preparation for several years. In December, I decided to live by that phrase like I had never lived by it before.

I had more than half a season of rugby in front of me. I also had a World Cup in the second half of 2011 in front of me, too, and the possibility of being in the Ireland squad and playing in some of the big games in New Zealand was something that I simply could not deny myself. Twice, I had felt the disappointment of being told that I was not being included in Irish World Cup squads. It could not happen a third time, I promised myself.

My body.

My business.

I had to start my whole season, from that point, from scratch.

Joe Schmidt had enough problems on his hands as he prepared to bring his 'new' club to the hometown of his 'old' club for one of the most important games of rugby in his coaching career.

I had to get myself right.

I'd never believed that coaches have to personally offer some form of 'counselling' to all of their players – it's not their job to get the head of every individual player right for every game. It's not Joe Schmidt's job to deal with my personal issues. He has his job to do and it's huge as it stands. I still thought that Joe had doubts about picking me for the game in Clermont. I thought he was looking at Hinesy as his No. 1, and that he saw Dev Toner as a young guy who had done a big job for Joe in the two biggest games of his Leinster career up to that point.

I thought that Joe believed that to be his best combination.

I tried to get rid of those doubts as soon as they surfaced but, no matter how hard I tried, I still had a recurring thought that I would not get picked and would not lead the team out at Stade Marcel Michelin.

I had told Joe that the game in France would suit me, and I told him that the game in the Aviva would suit Dev Toner.

In the middle of one of our conversations, however, Joe turned to me and said something which completely stopped me in my tracks.

"Mate..." he said, "Be careful with the Achilles. My career ended with an Achilles injury."

I looked at Joe.

Are you trying to tell me something, Joe? I thought to myself, as I stood in front of him.

Heineken Cup
Pool Two
Wembley Stadium, London
October 16, 2010

Saracens 23, Leinster 25

HT: Saracens 11, Leinster 12
Attendance: 45,892
Man of the Match: Jonny Sexton
Referee: Christophe Berdos (France)

—⚒—

Scoring sequence – 7 Mins: Sexton pen 0-3; **12:** Goode try 5-3; **16:** Hougaard pen 8-3; **20:** Sexton pen 8-6; **27:** Sexton pen 8-9; **34:** Hougaard pen 11-9; **36:** Sexton pen 11-12. **Half time 11-12: 45:** Sexton pen 11-15; **52:** Sexton try, Sexton con 11-22; **57:** Goode pen 14-22; **62:** Goode pen 17-22; **64:** Sexton pen 17-25; **69:** Goode pen 20-25; **75:** Goode pen 23-25.

Saracens: A Goode; D Strettle, A Powell (K Ratuvou 58), B Barritt, C Wyles; D Hougaard (N Cato 46), R Wigglesworth (N De Kock 46); D Carstens, S Brits, C Nieto, S Borthwick Capt., M Botha (H Smith 60), J Burger, A Saull, E Joubert (K Brown 46).

Leinster: R Kearney; S Horgan, L Fitzgerald (F McFadden 46), G D'Arcy, I Nacewa; J Sexton, E Reddan (I Boss 56); C Healy (H van der Merwe 61), R Strauss, M Ross (S Shawe 76), N Hines, D Toner (L Cullen 69), S O'Brien, S Jennings (J Harris-Wright 66), J Heaslip Capt.

CHAPTER THREE

"SOME OF OUR PLAYERS FELT ... THERE WAS A LACK OF RESPECT."
Vern Cotter

As I reached my mid-teens, I thought that making money would be more important to me than playing rugby.

I saw myself becoming a businessman, like my dad, and,after watching the movie 'Wall Street' I thought it might be good to be a stockbroker – though not exactly the demented Michael Douglas character, Gordon Gekko from that same movie!

But, making money seemed like a very good idea to me. I wanted to go to UCD, then maybe get to Oxford or Cambridge, play some rugby, and live in London for a while.

And, if playing rugby for Ireland fitted into that picture as well, then that would be great. I thought that would be the perfect life.

That's how I viewed things as I spent the final two years of my secondary school days as a 'boarder' in Blackrock College. Study-wise, I was slightly above average, but I studied much harder when I was no longer a 'day boy' and I also played rugby much harder and with greater determination when I became one of the senior boys.

As a junior, physically, I wasn't up to very much, to be honest. I could take or leave rugby. My skill level was high (why wouldn't my skill-set be extremely good, after playing 15-a-side games of rugby on my own, for years, halfway up the Wicklow mountains). I was on the Junior Cup winning team that hammered St Mary's in the final at Lansdowne Road. I was tall, but I wasn't one of the standout players. I was no Barry Gibney. He was our giant No. 8, and he'd get the ball and run over people all afternoon long.

And I became even lankier when I went on a family holiday one summer in Italy and discovered the joy of outstanding food! I did nothing but eat for those three months, and I must have grown five or six inches in total. The summer after that I threw in my lot with Kilmacud Crokes GAA club. Tom Keating brought me over to the club and, before long, I was getting picked at full-forward on the club's Under-16 football team. We lost to Erin's Isle in the Championship semi-final that year. But, when I started boarding in 'Rock, my Gaelic football career had to be put on ice. For good, as it turned out.

In my sixth year in 'Rock I shared the best room in the entire college with Bob Casey. He was the biggest man in the college, an absolute giant, and we quickly became best friends.

After dislocating my shoulder in fifth year, I got back for the final two games of our Senior Cup win in 1995. We beat Castleknock in the semi-final and, after being 8-0 up at half time against Clongowes in the final, having played with a gale force wind at our backs and with rain and hail for good measure, we set up maul after maul at the back of the scrum in the second half, killed the clock for the entire half, and won 8-3.

Nine of our team was on the Leinster Schools team which toured Australia that summer. This included Bob, Barry Gibney, Tom Keating, Peter Smyth, Dave Johnson, Malcolm Cuffe, Emmet Farrell and Ciaran Scally, and we were away on the trip of our young lives for nearly five weeks.

Also, seven of us were back for sixth year in 'Rock and we were labelled the 'dream team' when we competed in the 1996 Leinster Schools Senior Cup. Brian O'Driscoll was playing scrum-half that year and filling in around the backline but, to be honest, he was a bit small and we didn't take much heed of him.

Blackrock nearly lost to St Michael's in the quarter-finals, but we squeezed the life out of them in the end. We beat Terenure in the 'semis', and we played Geordie Murphy's Newbridge in the final on St Patrick's Day. Geordie was the 'wonder boy' of the Leinster Schools Rugby Cup that year. We won!

I was No. 8 on the Irish Schools team, which was coached by Declan Kidney in 1995, and by Keith Patton in 1996. We won the Triple Crown in my final year. Deccie was also coach to the Irish Under-19s the following season when I started college in UCD and he asked me to captain his team.

That was my first time to captain any team.

Jim Glennon was manager of the team and he subsequently played an influential role in my early career development, and also in introducing me to Leinster.

It was the first year of the Under-19 World Cup. We travelled out to

Argentina with a very average team. It was mashed together more than anything else, but I loved the responsibility of being team captain. We beat Portugal in our opening game and, then, in our second match against Scotland which was played in the most astonishing 40-degree heat, Tom Keating (the future Best Man at my wedding) got an awful bang and later had to have his spleen removed. Argentina absolutely crushed us in the semi-finals.

With Drico, Paddy Wallace and Donncha O'Callaghan onboard, Ireland actually won the Under-19 World Cup the following year.

My rugby career had taken off, or blasted off to be much more precise. Eddie O'Sullivan was coaching the Irish Under-21s, and I got called up to play in the final two games of the Championship in 1997. Brian McLaughlin, now Ulster's coach, took over the following year from Eddie and named me as team captain in 1998.

In that first year at Under-21, in 1997, I was two years younger than most of the lads and physically I found it very hard. I was No. 6, while David Wallace was in at No. 8, and we had a big victory over England in Greystones and went on to beat Scotland to finish the competition with two wins after losing the first two games I hadn't played in.

The English always picked the biggest lads they could find for their underage teams, and they still do to this day.

There was a great atmosphere in Greystones that day.

In 1998, we managed to win the Triple Crown by beating England again, this time in Richmond in London. In 1999, we had an even stronger team, but we managed to blow a Grand Slam by losing to Wales away, after winning all of our other games.

I loved where my rugby career was heading.

And, my pals and I had the greatest time of our lives for those three or four years. We had fantastic experiences with Irish Schools and with Ireland Under-19 and Under-21 teams and, meanwhile, at club level with Blackrock we were winning everything at underage level, every cup and every league, it seemed. But everything, as we had ever known it, was about to change.

The game of Rugby Union was about to turn professional and those old thoughts of walking the streets of London City, like a very tall buddy of Gordon Gekko, were soon gone ... for the time being!

I roomed with Nathan Hines in Clermont. We always had a lot to talk about every time we roomed together and, within a few months of him arriving in Leinster, we really got to know one another's games, and what to expect from one another.

I always roomed with either Hinesy or Jenno, and I found Nathan a really chilled out guy. He never got too worried about anything. He would float around before games and try to distract everyone else, but he would stay really relaxed at all times himself. He is your authentic chilled Aussie! He is also a great pro. Big into his nutrition, he took care of himself while he was with us, better than most.

When away from home, he liked to study and in Clermont he spent hours, it seemed, Skyping his wife, Leanne and young son, Josh. Occasionally watching him having conversations with his family on his laptop really gave a whole different insight and appreciation of the man, as opposed to the perceived tough, hard-as-nails character who wore the blue No. 5 on the field.

On the field, Hinesy is a pest, and always has been, and he prides himself in being one of the most annoying rugby players in the whole of Europe. Which is a good thing when he's on your team! Not so helpful when you are playing against him. Having spent so many years with Mal O'Kelly, it took me longer than most other players to get to know my new partner in the second row, to be honest, but by the time we arrived in Clermont in December 2010, we were almost like old mates.

He explained his situation to me and the fact that his contract negotiations with the Irish rugby union were not very positive. They were not keen to re-sign him at the end of his two-year contract because of his age and because of the World Cup at the start of the 2011-12 season which would have him on duty with Scotland and absent from Leinster for September and most of October.

Initially, I found it hard to believe that we would be losing him. He had become such a popular member of the dressing room in such a short period of time, and everyone in the squad had massive respect for him from day one – and, in truth, took it as a real honour to have a player of his quality amongst us. A bit like Rocky Elsom in 2009, I suppose.

It wasn't just his strength and aggression that had him in favour with the team and our coaches. Hinesy also has soft, skilful touches with the ball and he completely complemented our style of play.

But, in Clermont, he told me that it looked like he would be heading back to France. That was his preferred destination if he left Leinster and, having enjoyed a previous spell with Perpignan and being a fluent French speaker along with his wife, it was natural for him to return to one of the strongest French teams.

As we talked in our room, the night before we played Clermont in Stade Marcel Michelin, I found it hard to imagine that I might be playing against him in a Heineken Cup match in 12 months time or so!

The nine-day countdown to Joe Schmidt's heralded return to Clermont had been difficult. The weather was absolutely atrocious and the freezing conditions left us looking to improvise in our training schedule every second day.

It was definitely a challenge for Joe and his coaching team to get things done and, on several occasions, we headed out to Skerries rugby club to try to get some pitch work done. The ground was marginally softer out there. We used the gymnasium in UCD quite often as well, but mainly for walk-through stuff. It's a good facility, but it is too small for a rugby team and all we could do was walk our patterns at jogging pace. But, beggars could not be choosers, and we were thankful to have UCD welcome us in out of the cold.

Whatever else, the snow was good for team bonding – as grown men, returning to their childhood, the daily snowball fights also kept us all on our toes. The most memorable fight was in Dublin airport, the day before we headed out to Llanelli for our drawn Magners League game. We were stuck in the airport for most of the day. At one stage we were on the plane and in our slot, and ready for take-off, but the plane had to come back in again. With de-icing, we were stuck in our seats for three hours. A great big snowball fight was absolutely vital that day to keep everyone happy and somewhat amused at our predicament.

Brendan Venter said a surprise goodbye to Saracens at the beginning of December, a couple of weeks before we played in Clermont. He announced his return to South Africa, and the former Ulster and Ireland centre, Mark McCall, was quickly appointed Director of Rugby. I was delighted for Mark. He's always been one of the really good blokes in Irish rugby, and his coaching career was given a huge boost by getting the No. 1 job at Sarries.

They were two defeats down in the Heineken Cup by then, however, and it was not a situation he would be able to turn around. And we did not intend to give him a helping hand when he brought his team to the RDS in the New Year.

Joe expected a hot reception in Clermont.

People, undoubtedly, were happy to see him, and he knew everybody in the club and around every corner, there was a big personal welcome for him. However, on the field, we had no doubts whatsoever that we were also in line for a very hot reception.

We were ready.

Joe knew their team inside out. He knew their processes and their moods and, alongside their coach, Vern Cotter, he had been absolutely central to them winning their first Bouclier de Brennus in 99 years the previous season, when they beat Perpignan 19-6 in the final.

We were all growing quite familiar with Clermont, as we prepared for our second game against them in less than twelve months. However, it was clear to see that Joe had huge respect for his former players. Talking about them, he would inadvertently mention lads by their nicknames and, on occasion, we didn't have a clue who on earth he was talking about.

Joe had coached every man on the Clermont team, apart from Lauaki and Paulo. But, Joe even had a good handle on the pair of them, as he'd coached Ti'i Paulo in his New Zealand Schoolboys days.

He knew what Clermont would try to do. They were in top form, with a high-powered 32-25 win at home against Toulouse at their backs. But, basically, he thought that they were going to try to beat us up. Pound over the top of us! Which is Vern Cotter in a nutshell.

Without Drico, who looked like he might be out for several weeks, we had a big job on our hands. He'd suffered a hairline fracture of his jaw in Ireland's last game of the autumn series against Argentina. When word first came through that he was in trouble, I looked to move the team on immediately. It's vital not to dwell on anybody's injuries. Besides, when Brian is absent it always puts more responsibility onto the shoulders of other people, which is a good thing in itself, and means, ultimately, that the whole team has no choice but to step up a level.

Joe had shown faith in me by selecting me in the starting 15 for the game. He also left the captaincy with me, despite Jamie's return from International duty with Ireland.

I wasn't in the form of my life. My head was still battling with doubts about my form, and also about my body.

But, I was so happy to be leading the team out against Clermont in their own backyard. As tests go, it was huge.

And that's exactly what I needed. One massive and supreme test to see exactly where I stood and, once and for all, to see if I could overcome the mountain of doubts which I had been living with for far too long.

After Joe, I knew Clermont better than anyone else, and I'd played against them more often than anyone else in the Leinster camp. I'd played in their stadium for Ireland A, against France A. I'd also played there in the pool stages of the 2002-03 European Cup when we won 23-20 (they were back-to-back pool games then, too, and we won the return fixture 12-9 for good measure). I'd been out there with Leicester as well and, in total, I'd been on a winning team in two out of three visits to the Stade Marcel Michelin.

It's a city, bang in the centre of France, with the Michelin tyre company at the heart of the place, obviously. Like Toulouse, Clermont has now become known as one of the toughest grounds in Europe to get a result. The stands are very high and the stadium has a tight atmosphere. And there's this noise they make all the time...

They chant something like… "If you are not standing up … you are not for Clermont".

Something with that message in it.

It's a ground you enter with a personal sense of fear which you must control, and use to your own advantage. For younger players that fear can also be wrapped up in some uncertainty, and that's a bad place to be. The older you get, the more the uncertainty dies down, the more you know that you can soak up the experience and almost try to enjoy it.

Definitely use it to your advantage.

But, everyone who enters Stade Marcel Michelin knows full well that, if you do not get yourself right, and if you do not have your head exactly right, then you are going to walk into a real hiding.

It's impossible to sit back and soak up the pressure against Clermont because, eventually, they will wear you down and then they'll run over you. We'd nothing to lose by taking the game to them. We were top of the pool. If we got anything at all out of the game, it would be an achievement.

We had a run through in the ground on the Saturday afternoon. The game was on Sunday afternoon. We were sloppy enough. But, that did not overly concern me, because I saw that everyone was up for it, and the younger lads especially, Ferg McFadden and Eoin O'Malley, looked hungry and ready for a whole new experience in their lives.

The two lads deserved their crack at it. They'd played and performed very well in the Magners League, but there is a huge difference between the Magners League and the Heineken Cup. Actually, they are like two games of rugby played on two different planets.

Ferg, in particular, had to step up and take up a position which was new to him, because he is not naturally at home on the wing, and he was coming up against Napoliani Nalaga who has been one of the top try scorers in France for several years. He's a real flyer.

Ferg just needed to do the job asked of him. In a place like Clermont, like any tough rugby ground in France, it's mostly about getting the nuts and bolts of the performance right. Get the nuts and bolts right, and then take it from there. That's all you can do.

We stayed in a standard hotel, in some industrial estate by a motorway. The French don't do fancy in most of their hotels outside of the bigger cities. The mood was good.

I like to mix with everyone in the squad and I find that that also works for me personally because I'm naturally more of a 'roamer' within a large group of people.

With our injuries, and with so many of the lads coming back a little out of sorts from the autumn International series, Joe had said to the press that we were put together with "sticky tape".

That was entirely for Clermont's benefit.

We hadn't had perfect preparation and the weather had definitely knocked Joe's plans to one side.

We had to get something from the game. That was our first target. We'd watched Racing Metro against Saracens the night before our own game, and it was a big surprise to us to see them come away from Vicarage Road with a 24-21 win. I wanted Sarries to win all of their remaining home games, including Clermont. With one away win on the board, all we had to do was keep winning our home games, and try to get something from one of the other two away games.

The set-pieces were central to getting that vital 'something', and I was more meticulous than ever in planning our lineouts. With Cudmore out of the picture, they had us guessing.

They selected Loic Jacquet in the second row ahead of Julien Pierre, for his kick-off presence. It was also clear that Cotter was targeting our lineouts. With Jacquet, Julien Bonnaire, Thibaut Privat and Alexandre Lapandry they had given themselves great options in the line.

Bonnaire is one of their most favoured lineout jumpers, and I found it surprising that the calls were made by Privat. They certainly had me guessing and preparing a whole new list of strategies.

They looked so strong in their pack, and even stronger than they'd been in the RDS at the tail-end of the previous season when we scraped home with our 29-28 quarter-final win. The former All Black, Sione Lauaki, whom they'd signed since then, is a bit of a beast. And Ti'i Paulo at hooker is incredibly dynamic. They had amazing strength, everywhere, but at the same time we knew that they had not picked their most physical team to start the match. It looked like they wanted to play us off the pitch as well as out-muscle us, and then bring in more reinforcements to completely finish us off!

They had their Argentinian hooker, Mario Ledesma, on the bench. They also had French Internationals, Lionel Faure and Elvis Vermuelen, and the huge Georgian human wrecking-ball, Davit Zirakashvili, in reserve. All three of them had started in their victory over Toulouse, but Cotter decided on Thomas Domingo, Paulo and the Argentinian, Martin Scelzo, in his starting front row for us.

It was clear to all of us that Clermont had not selected their 'bully-boy' team to start the game. Though all of those same guys were on the bench. The surest thing was that we'd see them all, long before the end.

They had an early scrum.

Lauaki came off the back with the ball and we dealt with him immediately. It was Bossy who picked him up. That's why Joe picked Isaac Boss in his starting team. Bossy knows Lauaki well, and had played against him quite often when they were growing up together in New Zealand.

Joe was counting on that.

He knew that Bossy would not be intimidated by the size of Lauaki, and would get stuck into him early. Bossy is one tough man in games like that. Joe knew that, and Joe also knew Lauaki as he had also coached him in his home country.

We knew it was going to be a dogfight, and that made the whole experience even more exciting for everyone in our dressing room. We knew we would be entering a cauldron. And, more than anything else, we knew we could not let them get a head of steam up early on.

After three minutes, Shane Horgan went in for a try. It was an amazing start, but we were doing what we had promised ourselves we would do by taking the game to them from the start. From their body language, we could see that they had come out to take a physical stranglehold on the game and they seemed surprised by what happened. A bit shocked, actually.

The try was a bit scrappy in how it ended up, but we had taken the ball through a few good phases and, at the finish, Shaggy was brilliantly opportunistic, as always. The score came after some good interplay by Jonny and Jenno and, after Jenno's pass out was partially intercepted by Malzieu, Shaggy recovered the ball. The ball went loose, and he picked it and went over in the corner. Jonny added the two points. It was the perfect start.

The surprise on their faces didn't stay there for long. They were back at our throats almost immediately and on the restart their out-half Brock James was almost in for a fast try. We had to make some desperate tackles to keep them out. But they were quickly level, anyhow, after Rougerie fed Malzieu and he broke Jonny's tackle and went over. Parra kicked the conversion. Parra and Jonny also kicked a penalty each before half time, but 10-10 was good for us. We were delighted with that score-line.

However, the pitch was incredibly heavy. After playing on such hard, frozen ground for weeks, we were surprised at how soft it got out there. It dawned on me that they might have been watering it purposely so that it would drag the strength out of our legs. Maybe not. Most pitches have such fine grass and the modern game is almost designed for really firm surfaces, but this was an amazingly soft sod!

We knew we'd be well tired by the end. We also knew that the fight would only intensify in the second half and we reminded ourselves, over and over, about just how it would be for the second 40 minutes. The bullying hadn't even started. They would double their aggression in the second half, that was for sure, and we were ready to meet them head on.

On the Monday after the game, back in Riverview, Joe would give me a little bit of a hard time about some aspects of my performance. He actually called me into his office to talk about the number of penalties we gave away in the game, and specifically some of the penalties I gave away. I had pushed the discipline issue more than anybody in the build up to the game, so he was only making sure that I was practising what I was preaching.

On the whole, I had been very happy with my own performance. Him telling me off about giving away penalties only reaffirmed for me how absolutely precise and tough he is in his analysis of the game. I was happy that Joe was just such a coach, but when you are on the receiving end of sharpish criticism, at a time when your confidence levels are not all that high, it can be tough to listen to. Such is the nature of our business.

I had given away a penalty in the lead up to the Malzieu try. The referee awarded them advantage at that time, and in training we had been talking a lot about how a team is disadvantaged when they have a penalty advantage given against them. When you see the ref raise his arm, you automatically freeze ever so slightly. And that's what we did at the time. Clermont really capitalized on our slow reactions to get in for their first try.

I had come in at the side of their ruck. We were already on the back foot defensively at that time and maybe I was wrong to take the chance I had taken. It was a soft enough try, and we'd been a little naïve in our defence.

They scored their second try 13 minutes after the restart. Jamie had been forced off shortly before that. He and Seanie O'Brien had been carrying the ball bravely and taking massive hits from the very start of the game and, though the whole team was taking a bashing in standing up to Clermont, Jamie and Seanie were clearly the worse for wear as the game had intensified in its sheer doggedness. Floch scored their second try after side-stepping Darce and touching down in the corner.

Parra and Jonny traded penalties midway through the half, but the key moment in the second half for us was when Jenno had what looked like a perfectly good try disallowed. We'd made real good yardage and took the ball on. Jenno went for the try himself, and he got tackled. He got up and scored, but Wayne Barnes adjudged that Jenno had made a double movement.

That score would have brought us right back into it. The other huge moment for us in the second half came after a piece of inspirational play from Dominic Ryan, who had come in for Jamie. We were all shagged, long before the end. The ground had completely drained us and Clermont had done everything in their power to pummel us. But Dominic had fresher legs and his try-saving tackle on Malzieu close to the end was definitely our 'Tackle of the Season' (later voted by the squad and management).

We got our bonus point in the end with a 20-13 finishing score-line.

But, only just! Morgan Parra missed with a late penalty kick for them near the end, which would have deprived us of that point and left us heading home feeling really sorry for ourselves. It was so important to fly out on Sunday night, beaten up and rightly shagged, but with that precious point in our possession.

Joe was less happy than the rest of us. At the after-match press briefing, he told the assembled journalists that he was absolutely 'gutted' by the loss. He meant it, too. Joe had come 'home' to Clermont to win.

After the game, I had been delighted with the team performance, and fairly happy with my own contribution. We'd lost a lineout before half time which had left me completely pissed off, but, at the same time, we had them rattled for most of that first half. And we went into the sheds with the adrenaline pumping at a fair rate of knots.

We'd been very vocal coming off the pitch.

We were all talking.

"We've got them… They've got nothing!" I remember shouting.

I was trying to drum up confidence in the lads around me because I knew that, once we sat down in the dressing room, the realization would quickly hit home that we had the same, if not twice as much work, to do in the second half. I didn't want a single moment of deflation in our dressing room, so I'd started working on the lads as we were coming off the pitch at the end of the first half.

After the game, Vern Cotter accused us of disrespect. I never found out what he was talking about, or if our shouting at the end of the first half had been the 'disrespect' he was alluding to after the match.

Personally, I thought they were guilty of a lack of respect to us, because at the end of the game as we were positioning ourselves at the tunnel to clap them into the dressing rooms, they headed off instead of joining us for the routine after-match ritual!

I think they were all shattered and disappointed at the end of the game, and I think that included their coach. They'd expected to steam-roll us and, when they brought a fresh front five into the game in the second half, they expected to break us down and get some proper daylight on the scoreboard.

Six days later, when they ran off the field in the Aviva after the return fixture, they still refused to behave as they should have behaved, and only two or three of their players actually stayed back to clap us in.

Vern Cotter knew that if Clermont had any hope of topping the group, then he needed to have his team beat us twice in the back-to-back fixtures. Maybe he felt that Joe had beaten him in their personal 'game of chess' in the first meeting. Maybe he wanted to immediately raise the stakes before the second meeting six days later.

The game in Stade Marcel Michelin was barely over when he had made his comments. What on earth was he getting at?

"I think that some of our players felt that sometimes … almost … there was a lack of respect," he had stated.

"I think our players are a little bit aggrieved by that," he continued. "So, it will be an interesting old battle next week."

We had a quick meal after the game and got out of the place. A mid-afternoon kick-off has its advantages. Instead of the early hours of the morning, we were all back in our homes by midnight.

However, no matter what time I get home, I'm always a bit out of sorts after a big Heineken Cup game like that. Most players are the same. It's nearly impossible to calm down or switch off.

A long time ago, a gang of us got into the habit of going to Eddie Rockets diner in Donnybrook on the nights we fly home after a game. For starters, we're always starving at that stage. Nobody has a stomach for much food an hour or so after the game, we're too dehydrated, but, after five or six hours, we are all absolutely ravenous. A table full of chicken burgers and tenders is just what the doctor ordered late at night or in the early hours of the next morning.

It helps to eat and talk through all of the other results in the other groups, which we had only been paying passing attention to for the previous 48 hours. That weekend, as we trooped home from Clermont, Racing had beaten Sarries at Vicarage Road and we all had a lot to say about that.

Ulster had beaten Bath 22-18 in Ravenhill, which we expected, but, in the same group, Aironi had pulled off an incredible upset by defeating Biarritz (28-27) to mark down their first victory in the competition. That was something!

Northampton kept their 100 per cent record intact in Pool One with a 23-15 win against Cardiff. With a lot of chit-chat before the game about both packs, things obviously got over-heated. Five players were sin-binned. In Pool Five, Leicester went down by five points to Perpignan, and Scarlets made hard work of it against Treviso only outscoring the Italians by four tries to three.

Most of the talk amongst us, however, was about Munster and about Paul O'Connell, who, after all his injury troubles for so long, got a straight red card against Ospreys at Thomond Park.

That was Paulie's comeback game in the Heineken Cup after his incredible injury problems. Munster won but Paulie must have been left gutted by his sending-off, and he had every right to feel hard done by.

He was being tugged by Jonathan Thomas, and swung his arm back across Thomas's face. The referee, Christophe Berdos, told Paulie he was red carding him for striking, but, watching the incident, it was clear to me that there was little or nothing wrong with it.

It was ridiculously harsh.

It also sent out a wrong message. If you are holding someone back and you get a thump on the head, then it is tough luck on you, in my book.

In Clermont, the same weekend as Paulie was red carded, I had been on the receiving end of a fairly decent punch. We had a 22, and the ball was dropped off, and it bounced. As it did so, I held back one of their players. I didn't know who it was at the time. It was an instinctive reaction by me. I shielded him away from the ball and allowed Ferg McFadden to take possession.

I quickly found out the Clermont player was their Argentinian prop, Martin Scelzo. He turned around and caught me flush on the nose.

Fair enough, I thought to myself, but I also looked around to see what the touch judge thought of it. He wasn't bothered.

And neither was I, to be honest. I was holding Scelzo back, same as the Ospreys player was holding Paulie back. When I got the box, I knew I deserved it. If someone was holding me back, I'd swing at them just as quickly. Most of us who have been playing the game for a fairly long time, hate nothing more than being held back illegally from the ball. There's nothing more annoying, really.

Paulie didn't even get to use his fist on Jonathan Thomas! Interestingly, Scelzo didn't play against us in the return game against Clermont in the Aviva Stadium. The official word from the Clermont camp was that he had broken his hand. But, I never did find out for sure if he had sustained the broken bone in his fist courtesy of my face!

Heineken Cup
Pool Two
Stade Marcel Michelin, France
December 12, 2010

ASM Clermont Auvergne 20, Leinster 13

HT: ASM Clermont Auvergne 10, Leinster 10
Attendance: 16,106
Man of the Match: Julien Malzieu
Referee: Wayne Barnes (England)

—⚓—

Scoring sequence – 3 Mins: Horgan try, Sexton con 0-7; **7:** Malzieu try, Parra con 7-7;
13: Sexton pen 7-10; **25:** Parra con 10-10. **Half time 10-10; 53:** Floch try, Parra con 17-10;
58: Sexton con 17-13; **61:** Parra pen 20-13.

ASM Clermont Auvergne: A Floch; N Nalaga, A Rougerie Capt., G Williams, J Malzieu;
B James, M Parra; T Domingo (L Faure 71), T Paulo (M Ledesma 69), M Scelzo (D Zirakashvili
41), L Jacquet (J Pierre 50), T Privat (E Vermeulen 69), J Bonnaire, A Lapandry, S Lauaki.

Leinster: I Nacewa; S Horgan, E O'Malley, G D'Arcy, F McFadden; J Sexton, I Boss (E Reddan
61); H van der Merwe (C Healy 55), R Strauss, M Ross (C Newland 70), L Cullen Capt.,
N Hines, S O'Brien, S Jennings, J Heaslip (D Ryan 41).

CHAPTER FOUR

"THIS GUY THINKS WE SHOULD RESPECT HIS TEAM MORE!"
Leo Cullen

For me, one of the most historic sentences ever uttered in the history of Leinster rugby came from the lips of Mike Ruddock, one of the club's first head coaches in the professional era. It was early in the 1998-99 season.

We were losing 42-7 at half time to Stade Francais in the old Stade Jean Bouin and, as we all took our seats in the dressing room, Mike Ruddock took a good long look at us. I was twenty years old, and I had sat out the first half on the bench with my old school mates, Ciaran Scally and Peter Smyth. In the 75th minute of the game, Ruddock threw me into the game to replace Gabriel Fulcher for my very first taste of the Heineken Cup.

The competition was still finding its feet at that time, as were lots of young professional rugby teams, and, earlier in that same season, Ebbw Vale had 100 points put on them by Toulouse in a 108-16 massacre, which was the talk of every other rugby team in the competition.

It was foremost in Mike Ruddock's mind as he looked us up and down during his half-time talk and, staring down the barrel of a 42-7 score-line, he finished with his immortal sentence.

"I'm not going to be part of a team which loses by 100 points!" Mike daringly challenged us all.

As debuts go, mine was certainly inauspicious, but I did do my little bit in the second half to limit the damage on the scoreboard to 56-31 at the finish.

I was on a part-time contract with Leinster, worth the princely sum of IR£7,500 per year, which was a small fortune for a student in college when he saw a few hundred quid rolling into his bank account at the end of every month. I was studying History and Economics in UCD but, by then, my head was full of rugby.

Back then, the Leinster team was headquartered in a few portacabins which is such a far cry from the very successful professional club which is now in the hands of our Chief Executive, Mick Dawson, and has almost 140 people working full-time within the whole organisation.

I trained all summer with Leinster in my first year. I was a bean-pole amongst rugby players who were well moulded into all shapes and sizes from an amateur era. Most of the 'old' forwards were overweight and hated the fitness regime. On the other hand, all of us 'young' lads loved it. And then there were one or two others, like Trev Brennan, who took to the professional game like a shark to water.

Trev just wanted to bang into people all day long. I was nineteen years old. I had not played one senior game of rugby and, naturally, I was no supreme genetic specimen.

Ruddock loved lads like Trev. He wanted to establish a physical base for his team, and he'd flog the living daylights out of us on the field.

I was playing No. 6 and No. 8 in training with Leinster, and also with Blackrock, and it was Mike Ruddock who first put a screw into my head about playing second row.

I was still developing physically. In truth, I should have spent more time working on my physical development, and less time playing rugby. I was playing heaps of rugby. Far too much for my own good. But I was ambitious.

I wanted everyone to see how good I was.

I wanted a full-time contract with Leinster, and, eventually, I got one in my third year as a 'professional' on the club's books.

At that stage, my old school buddy, Bob Casey, was starting for Leinster. He had officially stepped in front of me in the pecking order. He was always way bigger than I was and, with a three or four stone advantage over me, he also progressed faster in those early days.

I became obsessed with getting bigger.

I knew I needed to be 110 kilos or more to get my career where I needed it to be. But, I was barely able to break 100 kilos. I needed to find an extra 10kilos. Then, when I did find it, it was like I was carrying a sack full of stones around the field with me in games.

Mal O'Kelly was No. 1 choice for the second row. I was fighting it out with Bob for the second place. He had toured in Australia with Ireland in 1999 and he'd got his first cap in the Six Nations the following spring. Meanwhile, I had spent far too much time on the bench during the 1999-2000 season for my own liking.

Things changed when Matt Williams was appointed Leinster coach. All of a sudden, Bob was on the bench. Matt saw me more in his plans. The 2000-01 season was the first year of the Celtic League. We won it, and started in Leinster's most famous win, up to that point, as a professional club when we defeated Munster.

Leinster were brave in Lansdowne Road that afternoon and, after being 15-6 behind early in the second half, we fought back for a brilliant 24-20 victory. And we did so with 14 men, as Eric Miller had been sent off early on. The game was also a lesson for me.

Mal and I faced Mick Galwey and Paul O'Connell in the second row. They had Foley, Alan Quinlan and David Wallace in the back row, and their pack physically dominated us for too long in the game.

I was taken off with 20 minutes to go, which was the normal course of events, with Bob coming in. In the final quarter we got a couple of tries, and we won, but I was part of the 'disaster' as I saw it for the first hour of play.

I didn't feel I had contributed as I should have.

I felt that I'd played pretty poorly.

I was part of the Irish national squads but I was not getting capped. At the end of the 2001 season I thought I might get my first cap on the tour of Romania, as a lot of the guys were off with the Lions that summer, but I damaged my Achilles and my ankle felt unstable, so I missed out. I had to get my ankle surgery instead. Mick O'Driscoll beat me to it and got his first cap.

Paul O'Connell had also got capped that season in the Six Nations.

Where'd he come from? I'd asked myself.

Micko and I had started an Ireland A game together that season and Paulie had been on the bench. He actually came on for Micko in the game. I could see that he was a serious athlete. That much was obvious to everyone with two eyes. He was raw and rough around the edges, but he was a serious physical specimen.

Paul O'Connell was two years younger than me, Donncha O'Callaghan was one year younger, Mick O'Driscoll and I were the same age.

Donncha had always been on the periphery of teams at national level and it didn't seem that his career was moving all that fast.

Suddenly, there were an awful lot of second rows around the place and things were getting very congested in the middle of the Irish pack. Mick Galwey was near the end of his career, but he was still around the place. Trev Brennan wanted to play a bit in the second row as well. Mal was there. Ulster had won the Heineken Cup a couple of years before and Gary Longwell was there. Paddy Johns was also still finishing up his career, and Jeremy Davidson, who had toured with the Lions in 1997 and 2001, still looked strong, even though he was struggling to overcome a knee injury. The three Munster boys were there. Bob was there. And I was there.

But, in Leinster, I still had to bolt down my position in the second row, first and foremost! Mal was not for moving. The harder I tried in training, the more he seemed to relax and look totally carefree. When it came to games, he was always in a league of his own and I was trying so damn hard to establish myself. I was trying too hard all the time.

But, I was getting there.

I was first choice but I wanted to be bolted securely into the second row for my club. At the end of that season, Trev Brennan left for Toulouse and Bob moved to London-Irish. After that, Mal and I were both 80-minute men, in most games.

The following season, I played for Ireland for the first time, against the almighty All Blacks.

I had never seen Joe Schmidt so fired up for a game. We knew that Clermont would be gunning for us in the return pool game in the Aviva, so Joe wanted to give us an extra edge.

One morning, early in the week of the game, he asked me what I thought about the possibility of asking Ronnie McCormack and John Fogarty to hand out the jerseys to all of the Leinster players.

I thought it was a brilliant thing to do. Not just for the Leinster players to have two of their own recently retired colleagues handing them jerseys, it was also a fantastic way in which to acknowledge two of our own who had given so much to the blue jersey. Both men were retiring due to injury.

Fogs had played 165 times for Leinster, Munster and Connacht in a career which spanned a decade, and he was forced to retire because of recurring concussion. He was part of our Heineken Cup winning squad in 2009, and he had earned his first Irish cap only a few months before his forced exit from the game, against the All Blacks during Ireland's summer tour.

Ronnie had played 53 times with us and he'd also played for Ulster and Connacht. He had to retire because of a neck injury. I had toured Australia with Ronnie in 1995 on the Leinster Schoolboys tour, and with Fogs in 1996 with the Irish Schoolboys.

They both appeared in our dressing room and handed out the jerseys to the players. But first they said a few words. Ronnie is a brilliant speaker and he filled the room for 10 minutes with a hugely inspirational and emotional speech. It was tough on all of us watching the two lads having to leave the game on terms which were not their own.

Their entrance and their speeches set exactly the right tone for what had to be done on the field against Clermont.

We knew that Clermont's visit to the Aviva was looking like a full house. People wanted to see more of what they had seen in the quarter-final of the competition between us at the end of the previous season. The game out in Clermont, however, had not left the squad in the very best of shape.

Eoin O'Malley had suffered a cracked rib while deputising for Drico in the Stade Marcel Michelin, and doing a massive job in the centre for the team. He was out. Drico was making a marked recovery from his cracked jaw but was still uncertain at the start of the week, and Jamie Heaslip and Seanie O'Brien also had question marks over their participation.

Jamie had suffered an ankle injury out in Clermont and, although he made it to half time, he had to be taken off early in the second half. He spent most of the week between the two games with his ankle in a protective casing. Seanie had simply looked for, and taken, a pounding from them out there!

I was looking forward to it.

It was my first time to play in the Aviva, and leading the lads out would be something special, on a personal level.

I felt better, happier, more confident within myself, too. I was surer than I had been the week earlier. I was looking forward to playing well. I was also looking forward to having a good cut at them.

The doubts were still there in the back of my head, of course. They had not gone away completely.

My body ... is it breaking up despite all my best efforts?

Am I just getting old?

Clermont had picked Pierre and Privat in the second row for the return game, and that surprised me because Jacquet is far more athletic than either of them in the lineout. He was named amongst the replacements. Their selection told me that they definitely intended to bash us about a lot more than they had managed to do in their own ground.

Julien Pierre starts a lot for France, but surprisingly he spends a lot of time on the bench for Clermont. He's very strong in his entire game. Thibaut Privat, however, is more of a solid customer. He's never, ever flash in how he plays – the lads in my own dressing room, when they want to pick on me for their own amusement, like to call me Monsieur Privat!

I spent most of the week reminding everyone in our dressing room of exactly what Vern Cotter had to say about us a few days earlier.

"This guy thinks we should respect his team more!" I told the lads more than once. Though, to be honest, I was still not quite sure what their coach was trying to get at during his after-match press conference in Clermont.

Respect?

Seanie needed attention on the field three times over there. He is such a massive ball carrier for us but they targetted him particularly. There did seem to be a growing animosity between the two teams. Loic Jacquet had levelled Jonny Sexton with a very late hit in the build-up to Shaggy's try, and that pretty much had told us what to expect from them for the remainder of the game.

They were also coming over to Dublin with their bully-boy team. We knew what they were about.

They are a huge team, but Joe and all the coaches reminded us that if we played the game at real pace they would not be able to live with us.

They thought they were coming over to bully but we were ready to blow them away.

Cian Healy was back in our starting front row, and he, along with Seanie and Straussy, can carry a ball harder and with greater pace than most players in Europe. Cian brings so much to the team when he starts. Seanie had serious trouble with his ribs all that week and he had to get some heavy strapping on him before the game began.

We knew the game would have that extra edge and, as a forward unit, we had to be 100 per cent in tune with that. Clermont, at all times, are a physical, confrontational team. They would look to drive through us once again.

In Clermont, we had done a lot of work on stopping their maul, which is such a strength of their. The second time of asking, we knew we had to get into them even more and dismantle them as early as possible, and not let them get any momentum whatsoever.

Besides, we knew, for all their talk, they had never 'travelled' all that well. Out of twenty-five away games in the Heineken Cup, they'd only won six of them, and they'd lost four times in Ireland. They'd never won here. It was our turn to do a big performance on them.

We had beaten them when not at our best in the RDS in the Heineken Cup quarter-final, and some of our lads did not turn up to play that night. That victory tasted a little bit like a defeat! Add that to the actual defeat in Clermont and it wasn't difficult to convince every last man on the Leinster team that it was time we showed Clermont what we can do on a rugby field.

The night before our game in the Aviva, I watched Saracens playing against Racing Metro in the snow in Paris. We were delighted to see Sarries win. That win evened things up again amongst the other teams in the group, and left us out in front and in control of everybody.

Sarries picked a young team and Racing had a few changes due to sickness. The conditions in which they played the game were also horrific, with the snow belting down. It was hard to see the touchlines in the second half. The game should probably have been abandoned but, all the same, it was great viewing for us.

It was just as cold in Dublin.

There was a great atmosphere the day of the game but the weather was absolutely freezing. We knew our marketing guys were trying extra hard to make the big crowd happy and keep everyone in the best of spirits for the rest of the evening. They had planned to have a giant Christmas cracker in the middle of the field.

And a Santa Claus dressed, from top to bottom, in the royal blue of Leinster!

Our people had a fun night ready for a huge crowd, which was an incredible performance so soon after the poor attendances at the autumn Internationals in the Aviva.

A huge hit from Straussy on Malzieu set the tone for the remainder of the game. It was a game they had to come to take from us.

Jonny kicked a good penalty in the 4th minute, but it bounced back off the right post. We didn't drop our heads. Cian Healy got in for a try on 8 minutes after great clearing out at a ruck, and threw himself over the line. They knew they had to come right back at us, and they did.

If we stopped them scoring at that point, we knew that we would be bossing the rest of the game. They would get the message!

Their full-back, Benoit Baby, opened up our defence with some tidy footwork, which was a touch of genius, and they got the ball into our 22 and wanted their try. A big drive from Sione Lauaki was just about stopped. They were on our try line and they probably should have got their try. We did not handle their maul at all well. They broke off the back on us, and had us at their mercy. We won a resulting penalty but it was a marginal call by Nigel Owens. He could have decided it either way.

Morgan Parra kicked a penalty for them and Jonny also kicked one for us, and we led 10-3 at half time. However, the absolute misery they had in the RDS with their kicking came back to revisit them in that first half at the Aviva, as Parra missed with two other penalty attempts in the opening 30 minutes.

We upped the pace in the second half. We said in the dressing room at half time that it was time to blow them away.

That's what we did.

Seanie and Drico led the way.

And Hinesy immediately had a good try disallowed. Nigel Owens knew he'd made a mistake. Everyone in the ground could see on the large screens that it was a good score and that Hinesy had not been held up. From the scrum which followed, however, we finished the job off.

We attacked to the right off the scrum and Cian rumbled his way over for his second try. He was unstoppable. This time, the score was sent up to the TMO, Derek Bevan, and he gave it the thumbs up, and with Jonny kicking everything on the night we were 14 points to the good.

Despite all the excitement and drama of the moment, I marked those two incidents down in my head as another lesson learned.

The lesson? Always demand the Television Match Official.

Later on in the season, I insisted on the TMO in some games even though I had no idea whether we'd scored a try or not. In the semi-final against Toulouse, when Jamie went in for a try, I was insistent that it go to the TMO. Same in the final against Northampton.

As we packed for the scrum which led to Cian's second try, we all heard the crowd's reaction to the replay of Hinesy's effort. They saw that he had scored. Everyone started booing Nigel Owens' decision.

Owens knew that he had got it wrong. And when he went to the TMO after Cian had gone over, I walked over to him for a little chat.

"While you're at it Nigel... " I said to him, "Any chance you can get him to have a look at the last one as well!"

To be fair to him, he saw the funny side of it.

They didn't look like a team which liked the pressure very much. A loose pass from Baby trickled into touch near their line and Jamie's quickly-taken throw to Eoin Reddan resulted in Seanie crashing over for our third try.

They scored their only try near the end. It came from Nalaga but, by then, Joe was already emptying the bench. We didn't get our bonus point, which was a disappointment.

It was still one huge job well done.

It was a mix of emotions for me afterwards, even though there was lots to be happy about. Drico was back and everything about him was important, his presence, his voice, his assurance. Ferg also showed well. We showed that we had the backs who can rip open any team, and with Seanie, Jamie, Cian and Straussy we also showed that we had forwards who are always dynamic with the ball in their hands.

I had never sensed a Leinster team with so much natural ability.

It was a good weekend for all three Irish teams, as it turned out. Less so for Munster, who lost 19-15 to the Ospreys in Wales, but they outscored their opponents by two tries to one for the second week in a row. If the two teams had finished level in the pool then Munster would have had the better head-to-head record. It looked to me, that Munster always know how to hold that slight advantage that makes all the difference in the Heineken Cup.

I still backed them to get out of a tricky situation, even though Toulon were in control of the group with a bonus point win over London-Irish. Munster required wins in their final two games, in Stade Felix Mayol and in Thomond Park. Ulster definitely looked to be going to the knockout stages for the first time since 1999, by completing a double over Bath at the Rec.

They would both have loved to have been in Leinster's shoes, however, as the weekend was a stunning success for us – apart from that loss of the bonus point! The 5-4 points haul in our two games against Clermont should have been 6-4. We achieved that, too, without Kearns and Lukey, and with Drico playing only one of the two games – and with Jamie operating on one ankle half the time.

But, the entire weekend was a big numbers game for everyone involved in Leinster rugby and everyone who has worked so hard to get the club to a place where we virtually filled out the stunning new Aviva Stadium.

The attendance of 44,873 was the biggest crowd for a Heineken Cup pool game in Ireland, ever.

And it was just short of the British record for a pool game, a total of 45,892, which was registered at Wembley Stadium for our game with Saracens. The Aviva crowd surpassed the full house of 26,000 at Thomond Park which has been the age-old record for pool games here. It also made mince-meat of the previous record crowd for a Leinster pool game, which was set in 2003-04 at Lansdowne Road, when 23,463 came to watch us against the Cardiff Blues.

It's good to put those numbers down on paper.

All of the people who work so hard behind the scenes in the Leinster offices had helped to create that magnificent night in a huge way, and they, too, needed to be rightly applauded for a brilliant job on the night and for weeks beforehand.

Whoever had the big idea to have the team's Christmas Party the day after we played Clermont at the Aviva must have been a confident man.

Actually, there were two of them. Jamie Heaslip and Cian Healy. They also decided on fancy dress, for the second year running.

It didn't bear thinking about … if we had lost to Clermont, we would have had to spend the next 24 hours mourning our Heineken Cup defeat dressed like a bunch of eleven- and twelve-year-olds!

For starters, I had borrowed some gear from my friend, David Chawke, and had dressed as the character Harry from the movie, 'Dumb and Dumber'.

We had a bus pick us all up at Ashton's pub at 5pm for a mystery tour, which was not at all mysterious in the end. The A team were coming into Dublin airport from a game in which they had got hammered by the Cornish Pirates, so we first picked up the dozen or so seniors from that squad who were also heading to the party.

It was players only.

No Joe, no coaches and no management.

I was a bit worried at first about arriving at the airport. The lads had a few pints onboard, but when we all got into the arrivals area we discovered a great crowd there, who recognised some of our party and wanted photos

Joe and me at the outset of the 2010-2011 Heineken Cup campaign.

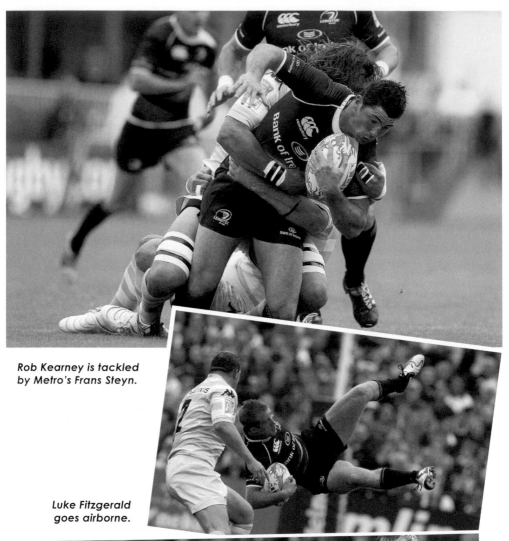

Rob Kearney is tackled by Metro's Frans Steyn.

Luke Fitzgerald goes airborne.

Gordon D'Arcy drives forward, supported by Shane Jennings, Mike Ross and Devin Toner.

Richardt Strauss fends off Lionel Nallet.

Isa Nacewa introduces himself to Sebastien Chabal.

Fergus McFadden makes it across the line.

Jamie Heaslip looks for space against Saracens in Wembley Stadium in London.

Even Drico has to be the 'water boy' sometimes!

Nathan Hines was someone who put everything on the line for Leinster.

Dev and I pass in opposite directions as I take the field.

Sean O'Brien tackles David Strettle.

Isa outstrips the same David Strettle.

The team huddles before playing Clermont in Stade Marcel Michelin.

Another day at the office: Heinke van der Merwe and I take the strain.

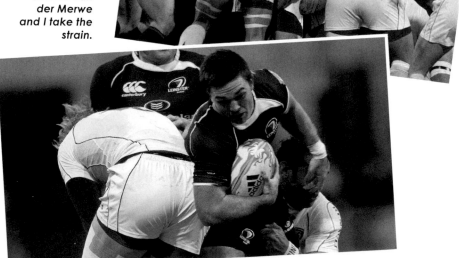

Eoin O'Malley tries to squeeze past Gavin Williams and Aurelien Rougerie.

Dominic Ryan is caught by Thomas Domingo and Brock James.

Isaac Boss manages to get a pass away.

Hinesy points out some of the game's finer points to me!

Drico makes a trademark run up the middle of the park.

Doing my best to pull a Drico!

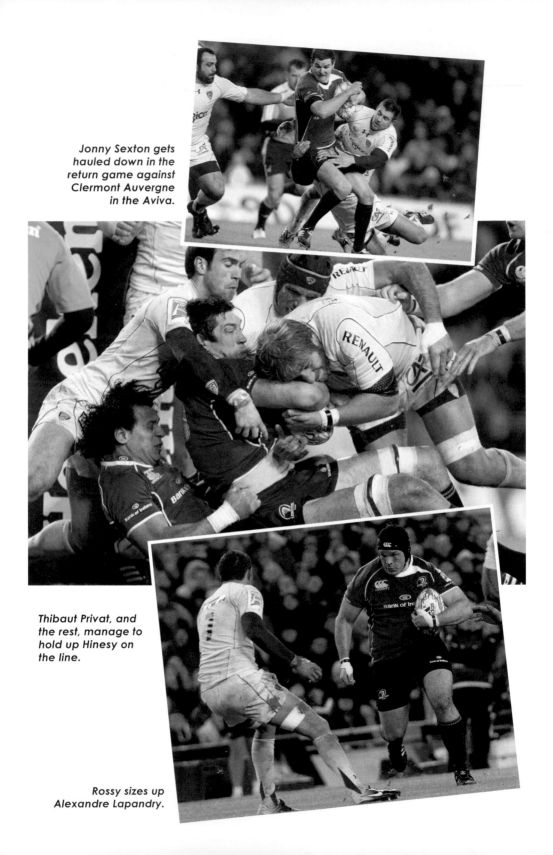

Jonny Sexton gets hauled down in the return game against Clermont Auvergne in the Aviva.

Thibaut Privat, and the rest, manage to hold up Hinesy on the line.

Rossy sizes up Alexandre Lapandry.

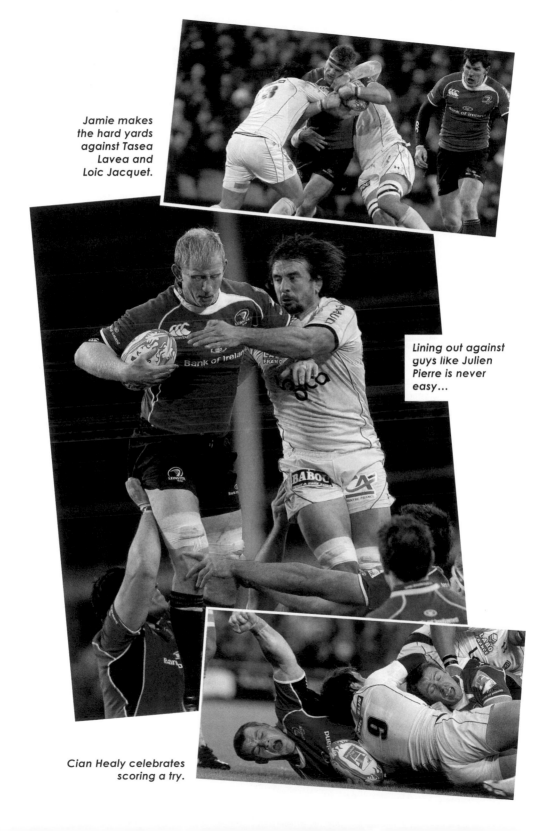

Jamie makes the hard yards against Tasea Lavea and Loic Jacquet.

Lining out against guys like Julien Pierre is never easy...

Cian Healy celebrates scoring a try.

I struggle with Steve Borthwick of Saracens in the return game in the RDS.

Shane Horgan attracts the unwanted attention of Schalk Brits.

Saracens don't give anyone free passage.

Seanie powers his way over the line for a try.

Drico is tackled by Kelly Brown.

Straussy and I get to grips with Hayden Smith.

Joe Schmidt chats to Jonny and myself in Paris ahead of completing Pool 2 against Racing Metro.

Seanie leaves a bunch of Metro players in his wake.

Heinke and Dominic try to catch their breath.

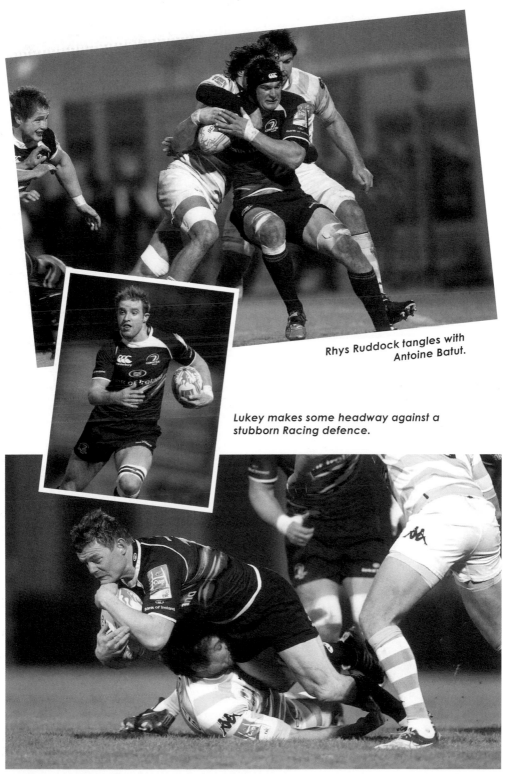

Rhys Ruddock tangles with Antoine Batut.

Lukey makes some headway against a stubborn Racing defence.

Drico hits the turf.

Jonny steered us out of Pool 2, the alleged Group of Death, and the best was still to come from our No.10.

taken with a Leinster team looking like a Leinster team should never really look!

My stress quickly died down.

A media disaster was clearly not on the cards.

We went to Carton House and then on to Mantra nightclub in Maynooth. Again, luckily from my perspective, both places were dead quiet. I could drink in my blue tuxedo in peace and quiet. But I had no intention of waking up in a bedroom in Carton House in the same blue suit, so myself and Isa Nacewa – who was dressed more conservatively as an American footballer – were in a taxi heading for home by 1am, taking a small detour into the centre of the city to meet up with some of my old school mates in Copper Face Jacks.

We had two games over the Christmas period to close off a year which, for me, was one I didn't have too many fond memories of, but one which I also hoped would give me the base to end my career as I wished to end it.

The third and final reconstruction of my left shoulder had done that, I hoped.

We had Ulster in Ravenhill two days after Christmas and then Connacht in the RDS on New Year's Day. Joe wanted to mix and match the teams. And, therefore, to beat Ulster 30-13 while resting some regular front-liners and follow that up with a 30-8 win over Connacht was not to be sniffed at. We did a session on St Stephen's Day in the big snow to make sure everyone was in one piece.

I had been with my family for Christmas dinner, first having spent a few hours down in the Blackrock clubhouse on Stradbrook Road where there is also some dinner for locals, and for anyone who might not have a place to go to celebrate Christmas Day. I go there every year to lend a hand with Margaret Browne and her volunteers, and it's a great, fun way to start the day. By Christmas night I was safely down in Wexford with Dairine and her family, the Kennedys.

It was hairy enough driving back up to Dublin in the snow, in the early hours the following morning, for our training session.

We had all been blowing hard early on against Ulster but, as usual,

Seanie put us all to shame with a barn-storming performance which included two tries. Isa had a 15 points haul in Belfast to put him up to third place in the league scoring chart, while Shaggy scored his fifth try in six games to prove that Leinster was still built on a few of us 'oldies'. Seanie had a rival for Man of the Match honours in Isaac Boss who was in no mood for losing to his former club. With 12,000 people full of festive cheer in a sold-out ground, Bossy was the most fired-up man in our dressing room.

I was rested for the Connacht game. Dairine and I went down to Youghal with friends for a couple of days R 'n' R on New Year's Day, and I tried out my shoulder with a good stiff swim in the sea. It was my best New Year's in several years.

I felt like a new man.

After five and half months of surgery and rehabilitation, and the action-packed few months which followed – when I had worried that my body was giving up on me, and I was consumed by a collection of doubts which I had never known before in my life – it was good to lick the envelope closed on a year which had, in the end, served me very well.

I felt that 2010 had also served Leinster very well.

The team was where it wanted to be in the Heineken Cup and the Magners League and was in a far better position than it thought it would be only a handful of months earlier.

Definitely, in Joe Schmidt, we'd found ourselves a new coach who had met all of our expectations and who was allowing us to try to become the team we had always dreamed of becoming.

Heineken Cup
Pool Two
Aviva Stadium, Dublin
December 18, 2010

Leinster 24, ASM Clermont Auvergne 8

HT: Leinster 10, ASM Clermont Auvergne 3
Attendance: 44,873
Man of the Match: Cian Healy
Referee: Nigel Owens (Wales)

—⁓—

Scoring sequence – 8 Mins: C Healy try, J Sexton con 7-0; **16:** M Parra pen 7-3; **38:** J Sexton pen 10-3. **Half time 10-3: 44:** C Healy try, J Sexton con 17-3; **51:** S O'Brien, J Sexton con 24-3; **69:** N Nalaga try 24-8.

Leinster: I Nacewa; S Horgan, B O'Driscoll, G D'Arcy, F McFadden; J Sexton, E Reddan (I Boss 57); C Healy (H van der Merwe 62), R Strauss, M Ross (C Newland 70), L Cullen Capt. (D Toner 62), N Hines, S O'Brien, S Jennings, J Heaslip.

ASM Clermont Auvergne: B Baby (T Lavea 73); N Nalaga, A Rougerie Capt., G Williams, J Malzieu; B James, M Parra (K Senio 66); T Domingo (L Faure 49), T Paulo (M Ledesma 43), D Zirakashvili (C Ric 73), J Pierre, T Privat (L Jacquet 64), J Bonnaire, A Lapandry (A Audebert 41), S Lauaki (E Vermeulen 49).

CHAPTER FIVE

"IT'S NOT THE END OF AN ERA."
Paul O'Connell

Michael Cheika arrived for the start of the 2005-06 season, just as I left Leinster and signed a two-year contract with Leicester Tigers.

Up until then, I had been part of a Leinster team which battled well in Europe every year. We'd kill some teams, and in our next big game we'd come unstuck. We flattered to deceive. That was the frustrating cycle for the Leinster team and our loyal supporters.

We enjoyed playing to Matt Willams's style and there was no doubt that we could match any team in Europe when we wanted to. But we could never grind out wins like Munster did and, when we played against them, we'd often be left scratching our heads at the end of the 80 minutes, trying to figure out how we had just lost the game.

In the 2001-02 Heineken Cup we topped our group, which included Newport, Toulouse and Newcastle, but were beaten 29-18 in Welford Road by Leicester in the quarter-final. Then, the following season, we became only the third team in the history of the competition to win all of our games in pool play – seeing off Bristol, Montferrand and Swansea in some style.

In the spring of 2003, we had the route to Heineken Cup success mapped out for us. Biarritz and Perpignan, both at home, to begin with.

We handled Biarritz with an absolutely professional display in the quarter-final at Lansdowne Road, winning 18-13 in the end, and showing the supporters who packed into Lansdowne Road that day that we were ready to really do the business in Europe. But, two weeks later, back in Lansdowne Road, we lost 14-21 to Perpignan in the semi-final.

Losing to Perpignan was as dark a day as I had ever experienced with Leinster.

When I compare how we prepared then, to how we count down the final week to an important game now, I have to smile. Now, it's all about being sharp and fresh through the final stages of the season, and we spend only the *most essential time training.*

Nowadays, our fitness team of Jason Cowman and Daniel Tobin spend so much time monitoring and analysing players' training loads. They ensure that we are always in the best possible shape come the end of the season.

There's no doubt we had the team. Everybody talked about our backs, and they were very good – Brian O'Meara and Christian Warner, and outside them Gordon D'Arcy and Brian O'Driscoll, Shane Horgan and Denis Hickie, and Girvan Dempsey. Matt's play-book was mostly all about our backs, but we had a good pack, too. Reggie Corrigan was captain. Then there was Shane Byrne and Emmet Byrne, Mal and myself, Eric Miller, Keith Gleeson and Victor Costello.

We had a great team but we never became the team we aimed to be.

The perception was that Leinster's front five were not dominating other teams, and there was quite a lot of talk, amongst journalists and supporters who wore all colours, about our lack of aggression and toughness when it really mattered. I don't believe people were being unfair in their accusations.

After leaving Leinster at the start of the 2005-06 season, I remember being in a hotel with my new Leicester team-mates and we were watching a Leinster game together. Amongst the Leicester players there was the very same perception. They saw Leinster as being a 'city team' and a team with a soft under-belly. Teams like the Tigers looked at us and they honestly and truly believed that, when the going got tough, Leinster would roll over.

It was a shock for me to hear them talk about Leinster. Especially, as I had been at the heart of the pack for the previous five seasons.

To begin with, when I had nailed down my starting position on the Leinster team, I was, in many ways, the kid in the room. I was not strong enough as a character at the time to enforce my views. And, in fact, the issue of our alleged 'softness' was never addressed. The elephant in the room was left in the corner, undisturbed.

We might be slated after a poor performance and we'd feed off that criticism as a pack and go well for a while. In time, though, the old traits would creep back into our performances.

It was hard to identify the cause of it.

The years passed.

I became a more experienced member of that same pack and it was so frustrating not being able to fully understand what was wrong and why we were on such a crazy, and too often uncontrolled, roller-coaster with our performances.

When Matt Williams left to take up the job as Scottish national coach, he was replaced by Gary Ella for one season.

However, our attitude needed to change and, until that changed, our performances could never be lifted up to a higher level.

When a group of athletes, in any sport, are continually being written off and criticised to a large extent – perhaps for several years, season after season – then it is quite natural for that same group to believe what is being said about them and sub-consciously revert to that role. We actually stopped fighting to break out of the mould in which we were cast.

When Declan Kidney came in, there was a real sense of excitement within the squad and he started to change things, seeking to change squad personnel, but, by the end of the season, the offer of the Munster job was something Deccie could never have said no to, and I understood that. I liked Deccie. I thought he did a good job in that single season, but he left for the right reasons, wishing to return to his family and to his own province.

We had finished second in our Heineken Cup group in Ella's season, finishing behind Biarritz, and we didn't qualify for the knockout stages. In Deccie's season we were, once again, unbeaten in our pool which included Bath, Treviso and Bourgoin. Our try count against all three opponents was 33-10. In the quarter-final we had Leicester in Lansdowne Road once again and, once again, we badly under-performed, going down 13-29.

I was out of contract with Leinster at the end of that season and negotiations had simply stalled. I think there was a belief that I was a 'Leinster boy' and that I would never leave the club. But, that was not how I was thinking.

Internationally, my career had stalled.

I could not see how I would get back in the picture with Ireland by staying with Leinster and, in my head, there was only one team I wanted to join if I was leaving Leinster and that was Leicester Tigers. There was some interest from some other Premiership clubs and there was also the possibility of going to France. But, in my heart, I wanted to go to Leicester. In my head, I wanted to go there, win some Premiership titles, be competitive for them in Europe, and show the Ireland coach that he had to pick me!

Leicester were probably the No. 1 team in Europe at that time, even though they had lost to Toulouse in the semi-final of the Heineken Cup.

I felt it was the right thing to do.

I could not see how Leinster were going to change as a team. There had been so much disruption with three coaches in three years. The club was such a massive part of my life, however, as I had played on Leinster teams since I was seventeen years old.

That was ten long years for me.

My Leicester contract arrived one morning and it was with a heavy heart that I signed it.

It was the first week of 2011, and I found myself standing in front of the Ospreys' captain for the coin toss, and I never felt older in my entire rugby career. They had a weakened team in the RDS for our Magners League game and perhaps we underestimated them because we struggled to a 15-10 win.

Justin Tipuric was captaining them for the first time, and I thought he looked fifteen years old – he was actually twenty-one and he is a very good back rower with a big future for himself with Wales.

We made damned hard work of it.

Ospreys had become a bit of a bogey team for us and they had really got into our heads by defeating us in the RDS in the Magners League Grand Final in 2010. On this occasion, even though they had a weakened team on the field, the game became a real war of attrition. Jonny Sexton got us out of jail on the night and converted five of his six penalty goal attempts.

Tipuric scored a try for them in the 16th minute, and they had held on for a 10-9 lead at half time. They soaked up the pressure in the second half.

We just managed the win.

Despite that performance, we had the strongest and the happiest team I had ever been part of in my Leinster career. And the entire squad was so well balanced, with experienced players and excellent, raw, young talent coming through in huge numbers.

All of a sudden, after Mal and Berch and Girv all retired at the end of last season, I find myself as the second oldest man in the dressing room behind Hinesy. Also, Fogs and Ronnie had gone. Stan Wright insisted that he was younger than me, but I'm pretty sure he didn't get his birth certificate until he was five!

We're a tighter group in every way. We're even tighter in our dress code. If someone had turned up in jeans a few years ago, nobody would have made a big deal of it. But, nowadays, we are more strict on things like that.

We used to be allowed to wear anything we liked to the airport when we were travelling to away games, so long as there was a Leinster top to be seen. With Joe, it's no more jeans. It's tracksuits if we're travelling and blazers after home games. The lads all responded positively to Joe's new instructions.

Though, a little 'help' in getting people into line is also necessary when you have such a large group on the loose.

Our 'Towel Committee' is still as busy as ever. That's made up of me, Isa, Stephen Keogh and Isaac Boss.

In a dressing room as busy as ours, somebody has to collect the towels and deliver them at the beginning of the day and, at the end of the day, somebody has to pick up all of those towels and bring them back for cleaning.

That 'somebody' is decided by the 'Towel Committee' and, in a fair and impartial way (some of the time, anyhow!) we ensure that if a player needs to be punished for a mix-up or some indiscretion then he is duly selected as 'towel boy' for the whole week.

We usually have a long list of sinners in a black book waiting for their week, and that week – I can say, having being there myself at certain times – is a real pain in the backside!

The week means the full week and, even if the player is not due to report into training on a particular day, he still has to turn up and be a good towel boy. Forty towels at the start of the day, and at the end of the day, five days of the week. If somebody has already done a week on the towels, and he still steps out of line, then the 'Towel Committee' has other ways and means of dealing with the offender.

And we do.

With a good crowd in the dressing room baying for blood, the offender is handed a giant dice which he has to roll. He might end up paying €250 to a charity, he might have to fill up the shower area with soaps and shampoo for the week, he might be expelled from the dressing room for the entire week and be condemend to the Academy changing room which is more of a cupboard, really, or, if he's really unlucky, he might have to turn up for training and leave every evening dressed in his No. 1s (which is a full suit, shirt and tie – the works!)

In the early weeks of the year, we also had a lot of our younger players in negotiations over their new contracts.

And that had also been on my mind.

It's always better if you can avoid having other clubs sniffing around your players. Jonny, for starters, had been out of contract and it seemed that every other club had huge interest in him. There was also Seanie O'Brien, Jamie Heaslip and Cian Healy.

I didn't want to lose any of them. But, even though I didn't believe that we would lose them, you are that little bit fearful when contracts drag on. Obviously, they'd dragged on with me before I decided to make my move to Leicester.

Cian was the first to sign up when he put pen to paper for a new two-year deal with the IRFU. The others signed, too, in the following weeks.

They are all central components of the team. Seanie had become one of the best players in Europe over the previous twelve months and has such appeal for Leinster supporters with his style of play. He also has his own supporters outside of Dublin, since he was born and bred in Carlow. The same with Jamie, everyone identifies with him and he's pivotal to the team. He came off the last Lions tour as one of the team's outstanding performers and he's one of the biggest assets the IRFU has on its books.

Shane Jennings also signed up for a further three years.

This was more great news for the province and for everyone in the Leinster dressing room.

Jenno has always been a vital component of the Leinster squad. Whether he is on the field or not, in the biggest games he is always at the heart of the squad. In addition, he is a neat freak. He is usually the first to ensure that the dressing room is being kept in order. Just as importantly, he also makes sure that nobody in the room ever gets too big for their boots.

He is one of the greatest competitors we have and he is generally our defensive captain when he plays. But, even when he is not out there on the field, he will always spend valuable time analysing the opposition threats.

Obviously, the fact that the pair of us lived together in Leicester means that we grew very close and I find him an invaluable sounding board for any issues which I ever have concerning the team.

We wanted to play with real pace against Saracens in our return Heineken Cup game with them in mid-January in the RDS. We knew that if we took the game to them that we would create lots of chances. It was also time to really lift the confidence of the entire team by putting in a big performance.

When you are at home in Europe, you want to run teams around the place and, ideally, run them ragged.

That was our No. 1 plan for Sarries.

I was coming up against Steve Borthwick, so I knew that I would have to be on top of my own game. He's a serious player, a former England captain, and he always runs a very decent lineout.

Sarries were a funny one. They were bottom of our group, which was a place they should never have found themselves, because they are not a bad team. They actually have a good scrum and a good lineout and their hooker, Brits, is a real stand-out competitor. He's a great ball carrier and has the ability to do special things. They can mix it up when they want to.

And, out on the wing, they have real flyers.

We found out early that Jamie would not be risked in the game. He'd taken a knock against Ospreys and had further aggravated the ankle injury which he sustained in our first game against Clermont.

But Joe had tried different back row combinations over Christmas. Seanie had a real stand-up performance against Ulster at No. 8 over the Christmas period, and with Dominic Ryan in great form at No. 6 and Jenno on the open side, we still had good balance in the back row.

Also, Kev McLaughlin was nearing the end of his seven months of rehab after his shoulder and knee operations. Kev had ruptured his knee ligaments in that Magners League final defeat to the Ospreys, and then he joined me to get his shoulder patched up with Len Funk in England.

We were so close to nailing down qualification to the knockout stages. Clermont defeated Racing 28-17 the evening before we played Sarries. That left us just one win and a bonus point away from getting there, but there was no point taking chances and risking further trouble for later in the season.

Every time we held possession against Saracens, it looked like we might score.

It was a phenomenal start.

We had two tries on the board by the 12th minute. Our recycling, our off-loading and our support play was better than it had been at any time in the season, and three of our six tries in a sweeping 43-20 victory came from the pack in the first half.

However, it was 3-2 in the try count at half time and each time we were under the posts we had to have hard words with one another. Everyone on the team wanted the ball and we looked brilliant when we had it, but there is another part to the game as well.

"We're not going to be under these posts again!" I had told the lads, after the second Sarries try.

We didn't defend hard enough and not everyone put in the work when Sarries had the ball, that was clear as day in the first half.

Our first try came after Drico and Isa created an opening down the left, and good support from Richardt Strauss put Seanie over the line. The second was a neat wraparound move from Ferg McFadden and Jonny, which set up Shaggy down the right, before quick ball and passes from Seanie and Isa set up Dominic Ryan for his first try.

Dominic got two tries in that first half.

But, before we completely ran away with the game, Short and Brown scored tries for them and, coming up to the break, we held a slim enough 15-12 lead. We became so loose and sloppy in the middle of the half, and when we turned the ball over we didn't do the job we are paid to do. Our transition from attack to defence was too slow and there was no intensity there. We didn't look like a team which wanted to defend at all at times.

Our minds were not sufficiently on the job.

It was so frustrating, because we were able to do it when we told ourselves to do it. Like, for instance, after their second try in the 33rd minute, when we stood under the posts and told one another that we needed another try before half time. Then, four minutes later, Dominic Ryan crossed for that try. It showed we could do it.

But, it was so annoying that we had to tell ourselves to do it. Dominic's second try was a pretty generous pop back inside from Jenno, when it appeared that he could have gone over himself.

Ryan is a serious athlete, like so many of the young guys coming through our ranks. He's got massive strength and he is a natural ball player. There's no doubt that he is going to be an outstanding player in a very short period of time. The race for places in the back row had heated up, which was great. With Jamie out, Seanie showed that he liked the look of himself in the No. 8 shirt. Kev McLaughlin had come back into the mix. Jenno was there – and being typical Jenno! Then there was Rhys Ruddock, who looked like a young guy who was only dying to get games and, like Dominic Ryan, show everyone what he was capable of doing when given the opportunity. Stephen Keogh was also pushing lads hard in training, even though he was struggling to get much match time.

It was clear that it was a really good headache for Joe and Jono Gibbes. With Jonny converting our third try, we were 22-12 ahead at half time but, in the dressing room, we reminded one another about just how dangerous Sarries were out there.

The big message at half time was to "Hold the ball."

That's all.

"Hold the damn thing!"

We are a far more confident team with the ball in hand than we were in 2009, and we have superior ball carriers in the forwards. Seanie was punching some serious holes from No. 8 and, quickly enough in the second half, we hit them with another good try. Jonny came back to the short side. He found Drico. Straussy made a great break and he put Ferg through for the try with a 30-metre run to the line – 29-12 gave us all the breathing space we needed.

Also, we could see the life had completely drained out of Sarries. They didn't seem to have too much fight left in them by midway through the half. They were not carrying the ball with any intensity anymore and an unbelievable piece of skill from Isa brought another try – though, in all honesty, their full-back looked like a man who didn't want to make the tackle.

Eoin O'Malley got our final try after getting a short ball from Jonny off a scrum. O'Malley is a strong guy and he finished well. The job was completed. On the scoreboard it looked to have been done in some style. Off the field, and in the video room the following Monday, not everything looked quite as brilliant as the final score-line suggested, however.

We had been thinking 'Next ball' and talking about 'Next ball' for months, but we were not living up to it for the full 80 minutes and that worried me. Winning the 'Next ball' and dominating the 10-minute periods either side of half time are crucial.

'Championship minutes' was what our former coach, Matt Williams, always called them.

No truer words.

By late on Saturday afternoon, we had said our good-byes to the 'Group of Death', and good riddance to it!

It was strange getting up for a game early on a Saturday morning. We've become so used to evening games and Sunday games but, with an early morning Saturday game (and we kicked off against Sarries at

1.15pm), you find that you are back on the couch watching other rugby games by Saturday evening. It's like being a kid all over again, playing early in the day and heading home to watch the sport all afternoon on the telly. I was happy enough with my own performance. The lineouts went well. It's always a bit of a challenge when you have a back row which is slightly on the smaller side. We had Dominic, Jenno and Seanie, who all play open side. They are competent lineout operators but it is not a central component of their individual games.

However, with Borthwick in my head, we had done such an amount of work earlier in the week that we got by just fine.

The game had a serious pace to it, but I was good with that and there were no problems with my Achilles for once. The doubts in my head had also been quietened down. Enda McNulty's reminder that 'My Body is my Business' was still working through my head and, every week, I tried to do something new to put that principle into action.

I was doing massage recovery and some extra yoga, reminding myself every single day not to forget about my body. I had to dispel the thought that my body was giving up on me.

Instead, I had to remind myself not to give up on my body.

I was surprised at how disappointed I felt for the Munster players I know personally, when I heard that they had not made it through in their group. The business side of me knew that it was a good thing that they were gone. It was better for Leinster not to have them in the knockout stages.

I could see the huge emotion on Ronan O'Gara's face when he was interviewed after their defeat by Toulon in Stade Felix Mayol. It was not the end for them – definitely not! – but it was the end of a remarkable record which no other team might ever beat in the history of the Heineken Cup.

Leinster had now qualifed from the pool stage for the third time in a row – but we would have to win our way through another nine groups, over the next nine seasons, to match what Munster had achieved.

What Munster did was so special. Toulouse may have won a greater number of Heineken Cups, but even the magnificent teams built by Guy

Noves were unable to match the consistency and amazing doggedness of Munster.

Toulouse have won the European Cup four times but they missed out on the last eight, back-to-back in 2001 and 2002, and also missed that train four years ago. Like Munster, Leicester have won the Heineken Cup twice but, for all their brilliant organisation, Leicester actually missed out on qualification in 2008 when they failed to qualify from the same group as ourselves – when Toulouse ended up on top.

I sat at home watching Munster play Toulon. I like to watch the serious games at home, and without too many people around, so that I can concentrate on what I am watching. Hinesy liked to tell me to my face that I am a rugby 'nause' and a complete nerd.

I knew it would be tough for them going down there, because they were not playing well, and Toulon are a team on the verge of doing great things. They had also been building their home ground into a bit of a fortress, as all great teams like to do, and a win over Toulouse was already at their backs.

And Toulon did come out of the blocks with all guns firing. There were less than 15,000 people in the ground but they had the noise level right up there, it seemed. Even before the game began, the home crowd applauded the rendition of 'Stand Up and Fight'.

The Toulon President, Monsieur Boudjellal had also stirred the pot all week. He was the man who had goaded Munster about being owned by the IMF, and he also accused Munster of calling his players mercenaries, which I'm not too sure they did.

That's not Munster's style. They have never needed to get into name-calling or schoolyard bluffing. Munster have waited to do their talking, season after season, when they got out on the pitch.

Basically, Monsieur Boudjellal did not feel that his club had received sufficient respect in Ireland, but I have always felt that respect is something you have to earn and, sometimes, it takes a long time. Munster have earned that. And, in Leinster, we've worked so bloody hard for so long to earn it, too.

ROG and Donncha O'Callaghan were both yellow carded, and Toulon more than matched Munster up front. In addition, Jonny Wilkinson landed eight of his ten kicks at goal. It was 32-16 at the finish, which made Munster's final pool game against London-Irish in Thomond Park a dead rubber.

Their first time not to appear in the knockout stages of the Heineken Cup in twelve years.

Absolutely amazing when you look at it.

Twelve years!

"It's not the end of an era." Paul O'Connell told television viewers, immediately after the game. "We're at a crossroads... We just need to find our way again."

Coupled with London-Irish's surprising 24-12 win over the Ospreys, which was their first win of any kind in over eleven matches, Toulon moved through to the last eight of the Heineken Cup at their first time of asking. Ospreys, like Munster, were also out. The two best runners-up spots in the six pools were out of their reach.

Northampton clinched Pool One on the Friday night. They whacked Edinburgh 37-0 and their winger Paul Diggin went in for four tries. They have a lot of young players finding their feet, and they have also built a strong team identity around Jim Mallinder. They were a team everyone else knew they'd have to keep an eye on, even though they didn't seem to have the same pedigree as some of the bigger-named teams still in the competition. But the manner in which they beat Cardiff back-to-back in December had surprised me, because I thought Cardiff would definitely take care of them at home. However, Northampton do have a great scrum. It has to be said, they absolutely annihilated Cardiff in the scrum in both games.

Toulouse went through as well, after Ruaridh Jackson led Glasgow to a surprising 20-10 win over Wasps in Pool Six and left Wasps joining Clermont. Munster and Ospreys were on the outside looking in at the closing stages.

Ulster, in Pool Four, had to wait one more week, as they were in one of only two pools which went down to the wire. They needed to beat

Aironi in their final game to grab a qualification place for the first time since they won the trophy in 1999. Despite winning in Ravenhill, they trailed Biarritz in their head-to-head meetings.

The other pool which would provide one of the two best runners-up was Pool Five, where Leicester and Perpignan were tied on 17 points each, and Scarlets were two points behind them.

Heineken Cup
Pool Two
RDS, Dublin
January 15, 2011

Leinster 43, Saracens 20

HT: Leinster 22, Saracens 12
Attendance: 18,500
Man of the Match: Sean O'Brien
Referee: Romain Poite (France)

—◊—

Scoring sequence – 7 Mins: S O'Brien try 5-0; **12:** D Ryan try, J Sexton con 12-0; **24:** J Short try, O Farrell con 12-7; **28:** J Sexton pen 15-7; **33:** K Brown try 15-12; **37:** D Ryan try, J Sexton con 22-12. **Half time 22-12. 51:** F McFadden try, J Sexton con 29-12; **57:** O Farrell pen 29-15; **59:** I Nacewa try, J Sexton con 36-15; **62:** E O'Malley try, J Sexton con 43-15; **80:** N Mordt try 43-20.

Leinster: I Nacewa; S Horgan (E O'Malley 60), B O'Driscoll, F McFadden, L Fitzgerald; J Sexton (I Madigan 69), E Reddan (I Boss 66); C Healy (H van der Merwe 66), R Strauss, M Ross (C Newland 66), L Cullen Capt., N Hines (D Toner 60), D Ryan, S Jennings (K McLaughlin 66), S O'Brien.

Saracens: : N Mordt; D Strettle (N Cato 64), M Tagicakibau (G Henson 33), B Barrett, J Short; O Farrell, R Wigglesworth (N de Kock 52); R Gill, S Brits (J George 66), C Nieto (P du Plessis 61), S Borthwick Capt. (J Saunders 78), S Wyvan (H Smith 40), K Brown, A Saull (J Melch 52), E Joubert.

CHAPTER SIX

The last week of March, 2003, was Grand Slam week.

England were coming to Lansdowne Road. Ireland had ten straight victories at their back and Eddie O'Sullivan was on course to land the country its first Grand Slam since the great Jack Kyle and the famous old boys of '48 had seized the most magnificent prize of all.

It's the greatest cliché in all of sport, I know, but genuinely you could feel the tension in the air as the days counted down to Sunday, March 30, 2003.

I had finally made my debut for Ireland the previous summer and I did it in a place where every rugby player in the world wishes to play for their country.

I came on as a late replacement in Ireland's second test match against the All Blacks in Eden Park.

We lost 40-8.

I can't say that the result really mattered to me as I returned to the team hotel in Auckland that night. We'd lost the first test 15-6 in Carisbrook. In the second test, New Zealand decided to send us home with absolutely no doubts left in our heads about our place in the great order of rugby life.

I had waited so long for my first start for Ireland but, thankfully, the caps came along in a hurry after that and I played in all ten of those straight victories before the Grand Slam decider against England. I started in two of them, including the slim 25-24 victory over Wales in the Millennium Stadium, which set the scene for the winner-takes-all meeting with the old enemy in Lansdowne Road.

I came on as a replacement in the eight other games but, in less than twelve months, I had played against Romania, Russia, Georgia, Australia, Fiji, Argentina, Scotland, Italy, France, and Wales.

It was the season of my dreams.

I was helped by the fact that Paul O'Connell's back had flared up on him on the flight back from New Zealand the previous summer. Gary Longwell was also injured at the time.

Mal was going to start against England in the second row. But, the week of the game, Paulie was back and up for selection. Gary was also back. The question was, who'd be starting with Mal O'Kelly against England in the Grand Slam decider?

I had a feeling I would be dropped from the team and the first 24 hours of that week moved along like 24 days! I was rooming with Victor Costello in the team hotel at Citywest. As usual, the team was due to be announced on the Tuesday morning in the team meeting room. If Eddie has not approached a player for a quiet word before that meeting then it is a pretty sure thing that you are either in the team or on the bench.

I'd been down for my breakfast.

Nobody was looking for me.

There were no conversations with Eddie or the team management at all. Those of us on the borderline of the Irish team know that there are days when you 'sweat' selection, and I had been in the 'sweating' category for most of my International career by that time.

When I came back to my room, there was less than a half an hour to the team meeting. I thought I was in the clear.

Back in the room, with Victor lying on his bed, I decided on a visit to the toilet. And that's where I was, sitting on the throne, when I heard a knock on our bedroom door.

Victor answered.

I could hear Niall O'Donovan's voice.

The door closed and Victor shouted at me through the toilet door that Eddie wanted to see me in his room.

In his room, Eddie didn't beat around the bush.

I was out.

Out of the team.

And, unbelievably, out of the match 22!

Very quickly, I went into a definite meltdown. There were tears in my eyes with the anger.

"There's nothing more that I can really say to you," Eddie continued. "I'm going with my gut on this."

I thought I was about to explode.

At the same time, I remember being in a bit of a trance and looking around Eddie's bedroom suite and thinking, This is a hell of a room Eddie's got! It was my first time in Eddie's room. The living room in which we were having our discussion looked huge.

What a room, I thought, and then I saw that his room was overlooking the fantastic golf course.

Then, Eddie started telling me that I needed to remain switched on during training for the rest of the week. He had told me earlier that Gary was starting with Mal but that there was a chance that Gary might not pass a fitness test. Paul O'Connell was on the bench. I had to stay for the week with the team.

After some time, I finally said to him, "But, you're wrong! This is the wrong call!"

Eddie had made his decision.

I shuffled back down the corridor to my room, where Victor was still lying on his bed, seemingly without a care in the world.

"They've dropped me," I told him. "FROM THE MATCH 22!"

My head was still buzzing with rage.

Victor stopped smiling.

He looked up at me.

"It won't be the first time ... or the last time," he said, matter-of-factly. "It's happened to me a dozen times ... you've got to get on with it."

History tells the tale that Ireland lost that game to England at Lansdowne Road, and lost badly, 42-6.

Obviously, over that period of time, Eddie had arrived at his own judgement about me as a rugby player. When Eddie made judgements he was not often a man for turning.

In June of that year, in preparation for the 2003 World Cup which England would win with a glorious dropped goal from Jonny Wilkinson in extra-time against Australia, we had an Irish tour Down Under. We played Australia, to whom we lost 45-16 in the Subiaco Oval, and then we headed to the islands and played against Tonga and Samoa.

Mal and Gary Longwell started against Australia and Paulie was on the bench. I was not in the match 22. After the Aussie game, most of the first team flew home but Eddie wanted to bring the remainder of us to the islands to have a last good look at us before he finalised his World Cup selections.

When we arrived in Tonga, our first thoughts were, how would we last ten days in the place? It was blisteringly hot. The air conditioning in our rooms didn't work most of the time and when we got it working it sounded like a motorbike.

The showers didn't work in some of the rooms either. Some of us washed in the sea and, occasionally, in the hotel swimming pool.

The food?

We survived on boiled eggs and chicken drum sticks – for some reason, it seemed that the rest of a chicken was not to be found anywhere in Tonga. There was never a chicken breast to be seen on any table. It was all re-heated drumsticks. Typically, with one day remaining on the island, someone found a fantastic little restaurant, owned by a German couple, and the entire Irish squad lorried in there.

Like the two island nations themselves, the two rugby pitches we played on were two different extremes. Paulie and I started against Tonga on a dog rough pitch in Nukua'lofa. We won 40-9.

In contrast, Samoa was beautiful and the hotel was absolutely perfect. But, it was even hotter in Samoa and there was absolutely no air to breathe as we started our game against them in Apia.

It was a nasty heat. The worst ever. Some of the lads lost 8 or 9 kilos in body weight in the game.

I didn't.

My shoulder popped out after twenty minutes, and I had to leave the field straightaway. I always believed that that was a critical moment for me with Eddie O'Sullivan as Irish coach.

It was such a tough environment those few weeks, and Eddie was in real Sergeant Major mood, letting it be known that we were in a place where only the strongest could survive. As I was forced out of the action, I believe that he had some existing doubts in his head about me confirmed.

I did the damage when I tried to tackle their speedster of a winger, Lome Fa'atau, who played for the Wellington Hurricanes and Glasgow in his time.

He was so fast, and with tatooes covering his legs, he looked like a painted train. He was one-on-one with me, and he stepped to one side as I made my dive at him. I caught the back of his leg and my arm went back, and my shoulder popped. I got it back in, fifteen or twenty seconds later, but the arm was completely and utterly de-powered.

The tour was over for me.

We played Italy in Limerick, in a pre-World Cup game and slaughtered them 61-6, and the lineouts went brilliantly. It was the best game I ever played in an Irish jersey, and in my head I was not borderline for the Irish World Cup squad. I felt I should not have to 'sweat' Eddie's selection.

But, of course, I sweated.

The squad was announced on a Sunday. So, Eddie was calling all the players that weekend and, on Sunday morning, I was sitting in my apartment in Blackrock when I saw his number come up on my mobile phone.

He told me quickly that I had not made the selection. This time, I quickly exploded with him.

He was going, like... "Listen!"

But, I was not prepared to listen to him for too long. I was so angry. Our conversation went nowhere, fast.

"Sometimes... " he said, near the end of the call, "you have to face up to it when other players are playing better than you."

"I don't believe that!" I replied.

In my head, I thought that I had done more than enough to warrant selection.

Before the start of the 2010-11 season, Leinster never had a scrum specialist taking responsibility for our scrum – at a time when rugby has become more and more 'specialist' in so many facets of the game.

Jono Gibbes had become our forwards' coach at the beginning of the 2008-09 season. He had just retired as a player due to injury and Leinster was his first big coaching job. He had played eight times for the All Blacks and he had famously captained the New Zealand Maoris to victory over the

British and Irish Lions in 2005.

Jono had led Waikato to the NPC title the following year, showing his leadership credentials by captaining the Chiefs for six seasons in total. Despite his young age as a coach – and Jono was not much older than most of the Leinster players when he first arrived in Dublin – his experience and strong characteristics made an impact on the squad from day one.

However, Jono was a back rower as a player and was not a scrum specialist. That role was taken up by Greg Feek when he arrived amongst us at the start of the season to run his expert eye over the machinations and the dark mysteries of the front row in particular. Also, Mike Ross was finally given his chance to prove himself.

With Harlequins, Mike had earned a reputation in the English Premiership as one of the very best tight head props in Europe. Cheiks had been slow to use him in his final year, but with Joe Schmidt there was a clean slate and Mike had quickly stepped up and shown that he was prepared to take responsibility for the Leinster scrum.

Against Toulouse, in our semi-final defeat in 2010, we didn't really have anybody taking that responsibility. We were caught cold by Lecouls, Servat and Human in their front row and, eventually, we were crushed by them and we had nobody to look to for answers.

A great scrum has to be driven by somebody in the heart of it. Mike spends massive amounts of his own time analysing other teams inside out, and in every game we have played this season everybody seems a lot more clued in to what we are doing and, just as importantly, what our opponents intend doing!

Feekie is a massive addition, of course. He arrived from Wellington during the summer of 2010 to work with us, and was soon seconded to work with the Irish scrum. With ten caps for the All Blacks, he initially moved into coaching with the Hurricanes and is just so knowledgable about everything he brings to our attention.

The most essential difference this season, though, is Mike Ross taking ownership of our scrum. It has a huge psychological effect on a team if you are getting drilled in the scrum and it has a knock-on through everything else you are doing on the field. It's not enjoyable, to put it mildly, playing in any game in which you feel handicapped in any way.

We're putting more emphasis on our scrums and more time into them. Scrummaging can be pretty laborious work, and monotonous, too, but you have to do the hard graft. You have to tick all the boxes.

Mike Ross is the man in charge on the field.

On the Tuesday morning, before we looked to wrap up our pool games in the Heineken Cup against Racing Metro, Declan Kidney announced his 32-man squad for the Six Nations.

I was back in, and happy.

As always, however, other players found Deccie's selection a complete disappointment. Coaching any team is one tough job, but coaching a national team is a job which takes levels of courage and self-belief which are of the highest order.

When Racing named their team for the final group game on the Friday evening, there were a lot of names we simply didn't recognise. We were left wondering if they were playing mind games with us.

With Top 14 games of greater importance for the remainder of the season ahead of them, I had secretly hoped that they might decide to rest some of their first choice players. But, at the same time, it's vital to always guard against any trickle of complacency.

Pierre Berbizier had his team second in the Top 14. His selected team had no Chabal, no Leo'o, no Wisniewski – who was suspended anyhow – no Bergamasco, no Vulivuli, no Bobo.

That definitely made the game look easier for us.

However, the last thing we wanted to do, after working so hard to get to the top of the group, was to turn up in Paris and let some team kick us around the place simply because we were not sufficiently well prepared.

Anyhow, we knew Racing would have big, massive lugs whoever they selected. It is the team they are, and it's the game they play. It's nearly all conservative, territory-based rugby from them, with lots of three-pointers as reward. They had actually not scored one try in the previous six matches at home in the Top 14.

All we had to do was play our own game, move them around and eventually run them off their feet. We knew we could do that. We'd already scored 16 tries in the competition, in five tough games, with eleven players sharing that try count, which was impressive by any standards.

However, like Clermont, Racing's pitch is quite heavy. The Stade Yves du Manoir is an old ground with ancient dressing rooms. We needed to concentrate on the task at hand and that task was to win one more game and guarantee ourselves a home draw in the quarter-finals in April.

One bad performance and, who knows, we could suddenly find ourselves on the road, heading somewhere like Toulon, who would be an incredibly dangerous opponent in their home ground.

Even having to get our heads around going somewhere like that would have been a disaster. Every time I saw them on the television during the season and saw them playing at home, I thought that was a place I did not want to have to visit. Their supporters are fanatical and their team feeds off the noise and energy all around them.

We needed to keep our heads and finish the job at hand.

That was helped with the return of Gordon D'Arcy after his calf strain. Darce was back to keep Drico company in the centre of midfield, which was good timing as Brian was celebrating his 32nd birthday that same evening. Isaac Boss, once again, got the nod to partner Jonny.

Jamie Heaslip was still ruled out because of his ankle injury and Rhys Ruddock was given his chance in the back row in the same week as he was called up to the Irish squad by Deccie. Everyone was absolutely delighted for Rhys but realised that it was a tough call for Joe to make after Dominic Ryan had scored his two tries against Sarries.

Who'd want to be a coach?

It was bitterly cold in Paris.

But, Paris is still Paris! For starters, they've got the best hotels in the whole of France. Staying somewhere half-decent, as opposed to some of the more basic hotels I've visited in the south of the country, was a good start to our weekend.

We were staying in the financial district of the city and, obviously, nobody paid any attention to us. We were actually able to go out into the middle of one of the huge pedestrian areas outside the hotel and walk through some of our lineouts without anyone as much as turning their head.

For the 24 hours before the game there were some Leinster players who were having their heads turned, however. There was lots of talk about the city and how cool it would be to live in Paris and play rugby there for a few years. Also, Michael Cheika popped in to the team hotel the evening before our game.

I was upstairs in the hotel in our team room where Mike Ross had, once again, erected a mini-movie theatre and we were watching the Christian Bale and Mark Wahlberg movie, 'The Fighter', which everyone had been talking about, and I only got to briefly say hello to Cheiks.

Friday turned into a long, long day.

The game was not until 9pm! There was so much wandering around the hotel to be done and, since it was so bloody cold outside, there was no great interest in walking around the city or searching out some decent place to have a good cup of coffee and unwind for an hour or two. We had all day, therefore, to think about the game.

It was going to be another game of bang, crash, bash!

They had so many younger players on their team, and so many other players who had been waiting around for a decent opportunity, that we needed to remind ourselves that it would probably be harder against a weakened Racing Metro team than it would have been against a full Racing Metro team which knew it had nothing to take from the game.

The first-choice Racing players would have been protecting themselves a little for what remained in the Top 14. The second-string players would not know the meaning of the word 'protection'.

In the cold air, and running around on their heavy pitch, everyone was blowing hard for the first twenty-five minutes.

We were struggling to fill our lungs. So were they.

The difference between the two teams, however, was that we were already three tries to one in front and looked very good to win the game more than comfortably. They came out to do some bashing alright.

Problem was, they were doing it far more recklessly than a team of first-choice players would. On our side, Sean O'Brien was naturally well up for anything they wanted to throw at him. He had broken their line for the second of our three tries, after Isa had first gone over, and before Jonny Sexton got his own seven-point score.

Their try, however, was the best of the bunch. From a 22 drop out, I tapped the ball down and their young teenage winger, Virimi Vakatawa, pounced on the ball and skipped by three tackles down the right touchline before scoring in the corner. He continued to cause us problems all night long, which was disappointing because he was one of their players whom Joe had especially warned us about earlier in the week.

Shaggy had sent Isa over for our first try, Seanie linked up with Bossy for our second and, four minutes later, after a good drive was held up on their line, the ball was shot wide to Luke Fitzgerald, worked back inside to Darce, and he offered Jonny the simple enough job of finishing the move off. It was 21-11 at half time.

We scored five tries in all, and Jonny grabbed two of them in his 21-point haul. The game was fairly competitive all through, but Seanie gave us so much 'go forward'. Bossy carried well, too. Going forward and being on the front foot most of the time always makes a game a whole lot easier, no matter who you are playing. Naturally, they emptied their bench as soon as they could.

With that, the second half became extremely niggly. It seemed as though they were looking for fights everywhere on the field. They also had a few decent drives, but we stood up to them well.

We finished the game without a hooker on the field and Cian Healy had to take over in that department. He'd played there a bit as a kid and, to be fair to him, he did a surprisingly good job for us.

I got involved myself with Nallet when he came into the game, and also Lo Cicero, but that is part of the business when a game turns ugly. It's pure business to meet fire with fire. We were also collapsing mauls and their crowd were getting quite pissed off with us.

Long before the second half was over, it was clear to everyone in the ground that we had the game well and truly won and, at that stage, my number one aim was to get as many of our lads off the field, uninjured, as fast as we could. There was nothing more being gained by us on the field. We did that and we earned our home draw in the quarter-finals.

We flew out of Paris that same night and it was 4am by the time we got to our beds. It was not even a night we could squeeze in a feed at Eddie Rockets.

It was strange on the flight home. You are still so fired up, and it was difficult to fully appreciate that we had half the job done in the Heineken Cup but that we would have a long wait before we got the chance to finish the job in the knockout stages.

It was perfect to wake up on the Saturday morning and spend the next 48 hours watching games unfold in all of the other groups. It was a long weekend of couch-potato rugby for me and, at the end of it, there was the drama of the quarter-final and semi-final draws.

We were through with Ulster and the draw held out the possibility of an All-Irish Heineken Cup final. But first, we had the two best teams in Europe over the previous decade standing in our way.

Our route to the final had us on home ground, in the Aviva Stadium, but we had Leicester first and then Toulouse (possibly, if they beat Biarritz) as visitors. Ulster had a tough trip to Northampton standing between them and the promise of a home tie against either Perpignan or Toulon.

All I really cared about was the fact that we were at home. In truth, if I could have hand-picked the draw myself, I would have chosen the pairings exactly as they were.

I knew the Aviva was good for us.

It was a new 'home' for our team, but also, playing Leicester and one of the French teams in the Aviva was excellent news for the Leinster organisation as a whole. The home gate is worth a significant amount of extra money for every team hosting a quarter-final in the Heineken Cup – while the home semi-final is a nice reward for the IRFU who share the gate with the ERC and the visiting team. Toulouse, for example, have gained significant rewards from winning home advantage in eight Cup quarter-finals and it is no accident that they boast some of the best training facilities in Europe.

Leicester, too, have built an impressive infrastructure on winning the big games on home territory, and they have an incredible record of winning seven of their nine quarter-final games in the competition.

So, if you get a home draw then you want to make sure that you are playing against the very best teams left in the competition so that you can fully maximise the effects of that home advantage. Better to play Leicester or Toulouse in the Aviva than have to face them in the Millennium Stadium in the final of the competition.

The sooner you play those kinds of teams the better, in my book. Besides, we were the form team. I knew that. I didn't need the bookmakers to tell me that we were favourites to win the Heineken Cup. Joe Schmidt had a winning team and his handiwork was all over the team performances, and no more so than in the try count.

We had scored 21 tries in our six tough group games, and only two teams did better than that, Leicester and Perpignan. They had scored 25 and 23 tries respectively, but they also had Treviso in their group, which afforded them a greater chance of hitting the top of the try charts.

My dad was the second youngest of nine children and, in February, the youngest member of the family, Maureen, passed away after a short illness. She was the first of his siblings to depart this world. Maureen O'Connor lived in Ventry, five miles west of Dingle, but she always remained one of Leinster's most loyal supporters.

The O'Connor home was a happy place for me during my childhood and we spent time there every summer. Maureen also had a son my age, Nicholas who died in a car crash when he was twenty-four years old.

As the two youngest members of the Cullen family, my dad and Maureen were exceptionally close, and she and my mum were best friends. Her illness was a huge blow to her family, but it also had a shocking effect on my dad and all of us. When Declan Kidney held an Irish pre-Six Nations camp in Limerick in the middle of January, I made it my business to visit Maureen and her family and stay over with them for a night.

I was delighted that I did so. She was a young woman, just turned sixty-one, and we all loved her dearly.

The circumstances of my visit to Kerry made it hard for me to get fully involved in the camp that week in Limerick. Having said that, any camp which does not have a game at the end of the week to really concentrate everyone's attention can be difficult and, at times, frustrating.

I had my own private emotions to contend with for the week, but I could also see that there were mixed emotions throughout the entire squad. The Leinster and Ulster players were all on a high after making it through to the Heineken Cup quarter-finals, while the Munster lads were on a bit of a downer.

There were eight Leinster players on the starting fifteen for the opening Six Nations contest against Italy in Rome. Admittedly, Deccie had a long list of names on his injury list, but it still showed Leinster's good form that there were eight players starting the game in the Stadio Flaminio, and three of us on the bench.

Luke Fitzgerald had fought his way back from his injury troubles to win the full-back slot and Ferg McFadden was named on the right wing for his first cap. Also Mike Ross and Seanie O'Brien were making their Championship debuts.

I would have loved to be starting but, after the roller-coaster ride in the first half of the season, with my rehabbing and my fight to find my true form, not to mention trying to re-ignite my confidence, it felt good being within the match 22. It's always great being part of an International weekend and it certainly beats sitting at home watching games on the television or the awkwardness of dragging yourself to games.

It was a funny game in the Stadio Flaminio and 'funny' not in a good way, from Ireland's point of view. We won 13-11 in the end but trailed them 10-11 in the 76th minute. Luke McLean scored the try to put them into the lead, but Ronan O'Gara, calm as you like, dropped the goal which put us back in front within two minutes.

They had scored their try straight after I had come on to the field.

I couldn't believe it.

But, there was no panic out there.

"Let's get our kick-off ... and get our hands on the ball!"

That was the calm order which we transferred to one another as we waited for the game to restart. I challenged the kick-off and, thankfully, they knocked the ball on.

It was our scrum. The ball went wide and ROG did what had to be done with the calm assurance of a trusty old pro!

We still had work to do, however.

In the final minute of the game they played the ball through several phases and attempted a dropped goal. All in all, it was a bizarre experience to have been watching the game from the bench, and then to be in the middle of such a dramatic conclusion.

It was helter-skelter stuff, despite the calm words which we were sharing around. We had to defend at the finish, and not give away a penalty – that is additionally difficult for a substitute who has just been introduced. It takes a while to get into the pace of any game.

Some lads come into games and because they have been fired up sitting on the bench watching events unfold they are instinctively wired to make some big hits. That's why, in so many big games, so many substitutes give away vital penalties. You have all this energy pent up for the guts of an hour. Next thing, you're into the action, everything is happening at 100 miles per hour. You can feel out of it! You try extra hard to get into the game and, suddenly, wham! You've done something you know you should not have done.

We held on.

It was a real escape.

On the Thursday evening after Rome, I went to the RDS to see Leinster play Aironi in the Magners League. We were in Irish camp but it was an evening off. We really struggled. They led 10-3 at half time and, although we were missing a load of front-liners, we did make damned hard work of it.

It could have been 17-0 at the change, because Niall Morris made a last gasp tackle to deny them a try in the corner.

In the second half it took a late try from David Kearney, and the sure touches and excellent kicking of Isa, to nail down a scrappy win in the end. Bottom of the table Aironi left the RDS with their first League point earned outside of Italy, so they were not too disappointed by the result.

Back in camp with Ireland, I was running a lot of the opposition plays on the training field and, as a consequence, I was watching the team very closely, almost like a front row spectator.

Even though we outscored the French three tries to one, we lost 22-25 in the Aviva, in a game we should never have lost. The big thing that killed us on the day was our discipline. We gave away far too many easy penalties and repeatedly allowed them back into the game. It's hard enough to beat the French, without opening the door to them every five minutes and handing them the momentum.

I thought we might have killed France that afternoon. But, the first half really told the story of the entire game. We got in front early when Ferg scored his first International try, but instead of building on that good work we were indisciplined and careless. We wasted good field position. We spilled passes and made wrong decisions and we coughed up too many penalties. Although we ended the half as we had started it, with another good try, this time from Tomas O'Leary, Ireland still held only a slim 15-12 lead at half time. It should have been much more, but we had given Morgan Parra too many opportunities of kicking points for them.

Rougerie did the hard work and Medard went over, unopposed, for the try which gave them a grip on the game in the second half. In the end, a try from Jamie gave us a chance of snatching victory and Sean Cronin was desperately unlucky not to be able to hold onto the ball with two minutes to go when he was hurtling in the direction of the French line with a try there for the taking.

I came on in the 80th minute!
I had been standing on the sideline, ready to come into the game, with three minutes to go on the clock. But play went on and on, without a break.

By the time I ran onto the field, the clock read 79:54.

Six seconds.

We had knocked the ball on, right on their line. I came on for that final scrum, which was the final moment of the game.

It might look comical, watching a player come into a game with a handful of seconds remaining, but I still had a job to do. I had to believe in my head that we were going to win that scrum.

I joined the lads five metres from the French line.

Everyone in green shirts was shouting.

"We need to whip wheel them!"

That's what the lads were telling one another.

"Whip wheel them!"

"No!" I said. "We need to drive through them!"

The lads were not listening.

"Whip wheel ... we'll get a turnover."

I thought we needed to try to drill them back and I told the lads a second time.

But, everyone was far too frantic.

The scrum was set.

It collapsed.

The scrum was reset.

We got penalised for trying to 'whip wheel'.

They kicked the ball dead.

A game which we should have won, hands down, maybe even with real authority, had been lost.

I walked off the field with my first 'six-second cap'.

I hadn't played an 80-minute game in almost four weeks. I needed a game. I rejoined Leinster for our Magners League visit to Cardiff.

Statistically, it was no ordinary game – it was my 150th game for Leinster.

I didn't pay too much attention to that personal landmark, as players don't think about that sort of achievement until they are well into their retirement. But, despite my two years away in Welford Road, I had joined an exclusive club. Only five players had passed that mark – Shaggy with 198 appearances, Mal with 188, Darce with 183, and Girv on 175. It was good company to be keeping.

The good news was that Stan Wright was back on his two feet for that same trip to Wales. He was called to the touchline in the 58th minute and replaced Clint Newland in our 11-3 defeat.

He had torn his Achilles tendon the previous August, and had only two and a half weeks of contact training behind him, but Stan is such an instinctive rugby player that he had no problem jumping back into the deep end. In his piece of action, he did his part on the Cardiff scrum by driving them backwards and forcing a turnover.

It was our first defeat in eight games and sent us back down the league table to fourth place.

Shortly after the game was over, I got a call from my dad to tell me that Maureen had passed away. All of her family and Mum and Dad had been with her in her home at the time of her death. Having broken the sad news, Dad told me that Maureen, shortly before she died, had been marvelling at the fact that I was getting my 150th Leinster cap. Sadly, she didn't make the second half.

Despite living in deepest Munster, my proud aunt had always flown a Leinster flag over her house, every single season, without fail. In ár gcroí go deo, ar dheis Dé go raibh a h-anam dílis.

The following week we got back on our winning ways, with a 30-5 win over Treviso in the RDS, with three tries but no bonus point. I wasn't at the game as I was away with the Irish team in Scotland. I missed out on camp for 48 hours at the beginning of the week due to Maureen's funeral, but Deccie and the team management were incredibly supportive of my need to be there with my family.

I was so thankful to them.

All the time, players miss out on family events during the course of the season, including funerals of family friends and relatives. We are used to missing all sorts of family occasions, from Christenings to weddings. It's part of the business of being a professional rugby player. The biggest casualty of all are the weddings of friends! That's not something any player would even think of asking permission for from their coach.

Missing Maureen's funeral was something which I could not have even imagined for one second. She had been such a kind and loving person in my life. Sometimes, rugby must come a distant second to real life.

Deccie knew that and understood how I felt and, to be fair to him, he was courageous enough in his decision making to keep me on the team bench for Ireland's game in Murrayfield. It is something which I will always appreciate.

I was on the field for 13 minutes against Scotland.

It was that sort of Championship for me: a handful of minutes against Italy in our first game, a handful of seconds against France, and a total of 13 minutes in Murrayfield.

Once again, the team had started the game very well and looked serious about taking complete control of proceedings and then, unfortunately, once again the indiscipline surfaced all over the field. We let the Scots stay in the game and, in the end, like Italy and like France, it was absolutely frantic out there on the field. Any time we got the ball in the closing 10 minutes we seemed to kick it aimlessly back down the field. The Scots were the team looking for the win. Instead of holding all of the momentum in the game, we handed them the initiative time and time again by offending at the breakdown, and, in that situation, Nigel Owens did what most referees who are simply human do – he started giving them most of the close decisions. Owens hammered us in the penalty count, 13-4.

Although we won the game 21-18, it was all defence at the end and that always takes so much of the good out of a game. It was a game which we had also won three tries to nil, and there was a gulf in class between the two teams for long periods. I believed we had a real chance of winning the Championship and making it another Grand Slam. We played such good rugby at times.

In the first three games we had outscored our opponents 7-2 in tries. The indiscipline had been a scourge and made the penalty count in those same three games an incredible 35-16 – there is no hiding from those numbers. The results confirmed that, and each of the first three games had just three points in it at the end. Ireland should have won all three of those games.

But we could just as easily have lost all three games.

The final two games of the Championship, against Wales in the Millennium Stadium and against England in the Aviva Stadium, were bitter-sweet for Ireland.

I came on in the 76th minute, to replace Donncha, in the Millennium Stadium. Then, in the 79th minute at the Aviva, Sean Cronin, Peter Stringer, Paddy Wallace and I all ran onto the field together. I came in for Paulie.

Naturally, I am always proud to play for my country and, even if it is just for a handful of seconds as was the case against France, I am proud and honoured to be the man chosen at that time. Nonetheless, it can also be frustrating to be reduced to such limited cameo roles. Less than half an hour of game time over the course of five games is tough, and it certainly limits the opportunity a player has to make the impression he wants to make, not just on the Irish team management, but also on the Irish rugby public.

We lost 19-13 to Wales. A combination of tough love from the referee, Jonathan Kaplan from South Africa, and the deficiencies in our self-discipline, led us into the jaws of the defeat.

There were other things. The Welsh try which finally won them the game had, as three of its key contributors, a sliced kick by Jonny Sexton with his first touch of the ball, a ball-boy who was too efficient, and a touch judge who was sleeping on the job. We had led 13-9 at the break.

Mike Phillips scored their controversial try in the 50th minute when he raced down the touch line to score after collecting a quick throw-in from their hooker, Matthew Rees. Of course, the score should have been disallowed, as the touch judge failed to notice that Rees had used a different ball to the one which had been kicked out by Jonny.

In my own mini-game at the end, there was the usual amount of drama. We had a chance to win the game. It was a last roll of the dice play, but we felt we had a chance. We created a two on one. Paddy Wallace went for it, however, and was desperately unfortunate not to get in for a potential match-winning score. It was a frustrating ending. It was also a sickening defeat.

Everyone in the dressing room was fairly upset at how we had lost the game. Deccie, however, did what Deccie does best when he had to front up to the television cameras and field questions which were fully loaded to get an emotionally charged response from him.

"We lost by six points," said Deccie, matter of factly. "It was a seven points decision!"

A few of us went for a wander around Cardiff that evening. Why not? Cardiff is always an entertaining city on the night of a game and we were in lousy mood, so we decided to try to lift ourselves. There was no booze onboard. We just wandered and laughed. The streets were manic and the characters who were out and about were entertaining.

The mounting frustration through the course of the Championship really came to a conclusion at a team meeting the week before we played England. Paulie spoke for some time, Drico also spoke for some time.

Everyone who left the room at the end of the meeting felt, for sure, that Ireland would have one of those outstanding performances in the Aviva. And, of course, we did. It's not every day an Irish team beats England 24-8.

But, it was more than that. It's not every day that an Irish team treats an English team as second-rate opponents. That was down to the level of confidence and aggression and composure within the team.

I wanted to be part of it so badly. Watching the lads play as they did, and wanting to be out there and share in it, was not an experience I would wish on my worst enemy. I came on in the 79th minute, finally. There was one lineout, which we won. Then the final whistle blew.

The Irish performance was built on a massive defence which, in truth, had been in place through the entire Championship. We had conceded just four tries in a total of five games, one of which was when we were down to 14 men, one from a missed tackle, one which had been 'illegal', and one against England from an intercept.

Brian O'Driscoll had given a master-class in that defence. But, in winning the game against the English, the honours were nearly all Jonny Sexton's. His quick tap and pass for Tommy Bowe's first-half try, which left Ireland 14-0 in front inside 30 minutes, was sheer brilliance of thought. Drico got the second try to break the Championship's try-scoring record after a superb pick up.

That night, I went out on the town and had a 'blow out' which was badly needed. It had been a couple of months since I'd had a good few beers. I needed it. It was time to put Ireland and the Six Nations behind me, and get back to business with Leinster.

I just wanted to get back onto a rugby pitch, and play.

And get on with it!

I'd waited and watched in the Ireland camp for two months. During that period of time, I'd also been waiting for the restart of the Heineken Cup, and our quarter-final against Leicester.

I was so ready for that game, and so ready to play the best 80 minutes of rugby I had ever played for Leinster. It was pure desire and hunger. I felt like a young man in the early stages of his career.

At the end of that week, I never felt more in love with Leinster and being captain of the Leinster team.

Heineken Cup
Pool Two
Stade Yves du Manoir, Paris
January 21, 2011

Racing Metro 11, Leinster 36

HT: Racing Metro 11, Leinster 21
Attendance: 8,326
Man of the Match: Sean O'Brien
Referee: Greg Garner (England)

—ɷ—

Scoring sequence – 3 Mins: J Hernandez pen 3-0; **11:** I Nacewa try, J Sexton con 3-7; **16:** V Vakatawa try 8-7; **19:** S O'Brien try, J Sexton con 8-14; **23:** J Sexton try, con 8-21; **38:** J Hernandez pen 11-21. **Half time 11-21. 52:** J Sexton pen 11-24; **62:** J Sexton try 11-29; **70:** B O'Driscoll try, J Sexton con 11-36.

Racing Metro: D Scarbrough; B Fall, V Vakatawa, A Masi, J Saubade; J Hernandez (M Loree 54), N Durand Capt. (F Steyn 71); J Brugnaut (A Lo Cicero 54), G Arganese (B Noirot 50), S Zimmerman (B Sa 54), S Dellape (L Nallet 57), F van der Merwe, R Vaquiin (J Cronje 60), A-H le Roux (A Battut HT), A Galindo.

Leinster: I Nacewa; S Horgan (F McFadden H-T), B O'Driscoll, G D'Arcy, L Fitzgerald; J Sexton, I Boss (E Reddan 63); C Healy (H van der Merwe 50), R Strauss (J Harris-Wright 47 – Healy for Harris-Wright 68-77), M Ross (C Newland 71), L Cullen Capt., N Hines (D Toner 71), R Ruddock, S Jennings (D Ryan 71), S O'Brien.

Chapter Seven

"There's blood down there ... do you want to have a look?"
Leo Cullen

I was twenty-seven years old and I should have been in the prime of my career, but I knew there was something wrong.

Finally, I grasped it.

I needed to re-start my career. I needed a change, a new environment, a fresh challenge, and all of that meant that I had to leave Leinster.

I was at a stage in my life where I had been on Leinster's books for ten years and I was very comfortable living in Dublin, too comfortable, perhaps. As a younger rugby player in Dublin there was always the temptation to enjoy life more than a professional athlete should, and it was hard not to spend time with my friends and join them for a few beers at the weekends.

I decided I needed to try to do everything differently and then see how my rugby career might look. Leicester had been interested in me for some time and I knew, in my heart, that if I ever did leave Leinster then there would only be one club I would wish to sign for, and that was definitely the Tigers.

When Leinster heard that I was moving, the IRFU came back to me with a counter-offer, but I had to explain that it wasn't about the money for me. I turned Leinster down and told them I was going.

When the contract papers arrived at my apartment in Blackrock one morning, I did feel a slight wave of panic. I signed them quickly enough and, within 24 hours, I had them back in the post.

I signed the papers without even setting foot in Welford Road, and that felt strange. I'd signed for Leicester but I felt detached from them.

What happens now? I thought.

I rang Leicester coach, Paddy Howard. He was really laid back and mentioned that there was a club barbecue for the players the following week and suggested I come over to be at that get-together. The International players on their books were slowly coming back to the club, and he explained it would be a good place to get to meet my new colleagues.

I already knew one of my colleagues, Geordie Murphy, so that was good! And, Shane Jennings had also signed up with the Tigers with me.

I arrived at the barbecue with a couple of light bags, including my kit bag.

It was a relaxed evening.

I had imagined that the club might put me up in a hotel in the city for a few weeks, while I scouted around to find a place to live, but that same evening I was told that I'd be staying in a general house which the club used for their players. It had three bedrooms. Jenno was also dispatched to the same house. One of their players was already ensconced there, and another player was due to join us the following week.

It did not sound like luxury.

I got the box room that first night. It was one of those absolutely tiny box rooms in a tight, three-bed, semi-detached house and there was not even room on the floor for my bags. The room took the bed, and the bed only! I have to confess, I sat down on my bed that first night and wondered what on earth I had just done with my nice life.

First thing Jenno and I did was get a car to share. Second thing on our list was to get an apartment for ourselves as quickly as possible.

It was hard over there, from the very beginning. It was full-on in training all of the time.

The Premiership kicked off and I got my first start against Northampton, which is the big midlands derby game for rugby supporters in the area. I was in the second row with Jim Hamilton, the Scottish International. Hamilton was young at the time, but he was a massive physical specimen, and he was also someone who was quickly improving his skill-set and reading of the game. He'd grown up in Coventry and had had a hard rugby up-bringing, and I found out that it was like that for a great many of the Leicester players.

The Leicester guys were naturally harder and tougher as rugby players. The whole club had a real 'salt of the earth' touch to it, but it was really hard-edged at the same time, which was clear to see every single week, even on the training field. Whenever contact started in training, they literally tore into one another. I had no option but to join them.

For the first few weeks, it was shocking to have to bring that intensity and level of aggression onto the training field.

I found an unfinished apartment close to the centre of town, which Jenno and I jumped at, and when he went home to Dublin the following weekend I made a few trips to Ikea and kitted the whole place out. The first weekend, with Jenno away, I had slept on the floor with a duvet. But the place looked quite good by the time Jenno arrived back.

With Martin Johnson exiting the club at the end of the 2004-05 season, I had imagined that I would be getting the opportunity of stepping directly into his boots, and trying them out for size.

It was not like that, either, in Leicester.

It was quickly apparent that Louis Deacon, who had come up through the ranks in the club, had been groomed as 'Martin Johnson No. 2'. Not me! Actually, I found that the second row was already crowded. Ben Kay was there and he had just been on the the Lions tour, while Hamilton was also looking to get his hands on one of the starting spots in the middle of the pack.

I had thought that I would be matched with Kay in the second row but, in those opening weeks, I discovered that Deacon was ranked No. 1 at the club, and the rest of us would have to fight it out for the second position.

So, it wasn't me and Ben Kay, it was me vs Ben Kay, with Hamilton waiting to jump in and join the action at any second.

That left my head spinning for those first couple of months. When we had played Leicester in the quarter-final of the Heineken Cup the previous April, it was Johnson and Deacon who started for them. I could not understand that at the time: Why was Ben Kay on the bench? Whenever we had played Leicester before that, it was always Johnson and Kay who started for them.

Kay was the starting second row for England and he had been chosen by the Lions. I thought he was the main man. But, obviously, I had got things completely muddled up in my brain.

I had to get my head around the Leicester way.

After the first game against Northampton, I held my place for the next Premiership game against Wasps and I had a complete and total shocker of a performance.

At the team meeting on the Monday after that game, I got to know Richard Cockerill – who was then the club's forwards' coach – for the first time. He aimed both barrels and, when he was finished, I was handed a trip up the motorway to Newcastle with the club's A team for a Monday night game. Four hours up and four hours back, that same night!

I watched Leicester play Bath the day before, and Cockers went with Kay and Deacon. He wanted his English boys to go up against Borthwick and Grewcock, in an all-English battle.

I captained the A team that Monday night. It was full of young kids and academy players whom I didn't know from Adam. We won. It was the first of two A games I played that first season with Leicester, but the first time of asking was a real grounding experience. When I finally put my head on my pillow at 3.30am on Tuesday morning, I knew for sure that my life had changed 100 per cent from the life I had been happily living in the comfortable surroundings of the Leinster dressing room.

But, I was still very happy with my decision. I understood what I was doing, and I never forgot why I was doing it. I wanted to show the people in Leicester what I was made of, and then, with a Leicester team which was chasing Premiership titles and Heineken Cups, I wanted to show, for certain, that I should be on the Irish team.

That was the plan.

I had to stick with that plan and make it happen. The season rolled on very fast. Hamilton got pushed back to the seconds. Deacon, Kay and myself were first-choice, all three of us! And it became apparent that we would be role-sharing.

In the Heineken Cup that season, we topped our group which included Stade Francais, Ospreys and Clermont but, in the quarter-final which was played at Walkers Stadium in the city, we got surprisingly turned over by Bath, 12-15. They were down to 13 men at one stage, and we dominated the game but could not get the points on the board.

My family were over for that game and everyone returned with me to my new home afterwards where we sat down to watch what was happening in the other quarter-finals – and specifically what was going on in the Stade de Toulouse where Leinster were in at the deep end.

Leinster delivered that majestic performance which is still talked about to this day, running in tries from all over the place, and shocking Toulouse with a remarkable 41-35 victory.

That evening, with my family and Dairine sitting around me in Leicester city centre, I privately questioned my great plan. Dairine's parents, Jerome and Deirdre, happened to be in Toulouse supporting Leinster – obviously, they knew the right team to back that weekend!

The following season, Leicester were drawn with Munster, and also Cardiff and Bourgoin, in the group stages of the Heineken Cup.

Our visit to Thomond Park was one of the most memorable moments in my two years with Leicester. Munster had already qualified for the knockout stages, but the winner of the game would take the group. It was the first time Munster were beaten in a Heineken Cup game in their famous old fortress, and I started the game with Louis Deacon, with Ben Kay on the bench.

Deacon is a great player and, at the time, I could see first-hand why Leicester liked him so much. He was a complete and total workhorse for them and got through a phenomenal amount in a game. Ben Kay, on the other hand, did more of the stand-out things on the team. Deacon was nuts and bolts. And I was developing into more of a nuts and bolts player, too. Leicester was doing that for me.

In the summer of 2006, my plan was still not flowering. I was chosen in the Irish squad which toured New Zealand and Australia in June and it was a decent tour, narrowly losing the two tests to the All Blacks 34-23 and 27-17, and losing to Australia 37-15, but I did not get to play for one minute.

I was proud of what I did with Leicester. I'd got plenty of game time and I captained the team fifteen times, which was an incredible honour in itself. I played in a Premiership final which we won with an overwhelming 44-16 victory over Gloucester at Twickenham. We were targetting 'The Treble' that season, and it looked so good.

We had also beaten Ospreys 41-35 at Twickenham in the EDF Energy Cup final. Though that season also ended in some disappointment when, with the Munster scalp in Thomond Park in our back pockets, we powered our way through to the knockout stages of the Heineken Cup, beating Stade Francais in the quarter-final at Welford Road 21-20, and then bringing Llanelli Scarlets to Walkers Stadium for the semi-final where we fairly cut through them for a 33-17 victory (when Jenno scored a brilliant individual try). It was Wasps in the final.

We had beaten Wasps by something like 40 points in the Premiership at Welford Road three weeks earlier and, as a result of that, we did not get our heads properly screwed on for our third 'final' appearance of the season, back in Twickers again. Lawrence Dallaglio was finishing up his glittering career and everything came together for Wasps, and for Dallaglio, on the day – and we didn't play. They won 25-9.

I had decided halfway through that second season to come back to Leinster, even though a part of me wanted to stay with Leicester and win that Heineken Cup with them.

I had the highest respect for my coaches and team management in Leicester and the club was the most professional rugby organisation I had ever known, at that time.

I still feel I owe the club a great deal.

However, I had met Michael Cheika earlier that year and I liked what he was doing with Leinster.

It was time to come home.

On Friday, March 4, I experienced something which has become known in the Leinster dressing room as Leo's 'Bloodgate'.

There was a lot of blood.

And more blood!

And, worst of all, the blood was coming from a place where most men just don't want to look. At first, I was slow to look myself but, when I discovered what had happened, in some shock and disbelief I've got to say, I asked a number of people in the RDS if they wanted to have a look as well, including the unfortunate referee, Andrew Macpherson from Scotland.

I was back with Leinster for one game, one week before we finished the Six Nations campaign against Wales and England. Jonny Sexton and I were allowed to play a game in order to keep sharp and I was delighted to be back and looked forward to playing as much rugby as I could after sitting on the bench for far too long.

We were playing Llanelli Scarlets on the night of Bloodgate in a fairly important Magners League game between the third and fourth placed teams.

At the start of the night, I wanted four tries and a bonus point to really drive us forward for a place in the knockout stages of the League. But, suddenly, midway through the first half, League points were of very little interest to me.

Shane Jennings had always warned me, usually with a few guys within earshot, that I would lose my balls one day if I continued tackling the way I tackled by wrapping guys around the front.

In the 25th minute of the game against Llanelli, I was trekking across the pitch looking to put a tackle in, when the young Scarlets' winger, George North, came within my range. He is a powerful young man, with serious leg drive, and I knew I had to hit him hard in order to halt his progress. I tackled him square on, as usual for me, and wrapped him up.

Then, I fell onto my back.

He was much stronger than I had imagined and I had been unable to hold him up in the tackle. His legs were still pumping hard, and as I landed on the ground he stood straight down on my balls.

It was a complete accident on his part.

The pain was instant and searing.

It was the worst burning sensation I had ever experienced, but the game went on, and I was back on my feet soon enough and following the game.

The burning feeling continued.

I hadn't had time to examine myself and see if there was any damage done, as I always wear cycling shorts underneath my rugby shorts and, in order to have a good look, I would have needed to avail of a timeout.

There was a lineout on our 22.

We were going to have a fast throw but the referee blew up the action because somebody else was injured at the other end of the field. It was time for me to look. It still hurt and the burning sensation had not ceased.

There was a lot of blood.

It felt like the blood was gushing and I didn't look properly at first. I didn't want to, not really.

I decided to have a second good look down there.

I was shocked.

I could not believe what I had seen. There appeared to be an eye-ball looking right back up at me.

"Fuck... !"

That's all I could say.

Then I had to think.

Was that my ball outside of my sac? I asked myself.

I investigated a third time and, this time, I dipped my hand right into my shorts and actually took my ball into my hand.

The sac was cut wide open. There was a clear split. I still had my hand in my shorts holding my ball when James Allen, one of our physios, arrived beside me. I looked at him, wondering what I should say to him.

"James ... you'll have to have a look at this!" I said.

James looked inside my shorts.

"Oh... Jesus Christ!" he exclaimed.

Our team doctor that night was Jim McShane and when he ran in I also invited him to take a good look.

"You'll have to have a look at this ... my ... " and I didn't know what to say next to him.

Next thing, the referee walked up to me. I bet he wished he didn't because I also issued the same invitation to him.

"There's blood down there!" I said to the referee. "Do you want to have a look?" By then, the injury was not horrifically sore but the burning remained as intense as the first minute it happened.

I actually thought of Buck Shelford for a moment, as I stood there on the field, waiting. The mighty All Blacks No. 8 had been in a similar predicament to me in the mid-'80s but, at the time, he was in the middle of one of the most famous and fiercest rugby games ever played. That test match between New Zealand and France was immediately re-christened the 'Battle of Nantes' because of what occured on the field of play.

Shelford was caught at the bottom of a ruck, where an errant French boot made contact with his groin area. His scrotum was ripped open and

Leinster fans get ready for the quarter-final against Leicester Tigers in the Aviva.

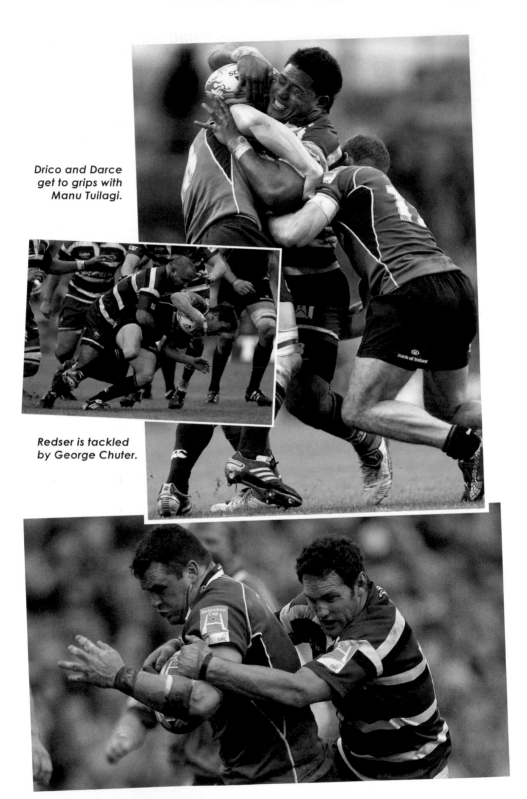

Drico and Darce get to grips with Manu Tuilagi.

Redser is tackled by George Chuter.

Cian is detained by Craig Newby.

*I get the ball away
in a hurry.*

*Drico tries to avoid
Alex Tuilagi.*

Rossy holds off the attentions of Ben Youngs.

Trying to take down Thomas Waldrom.

Shaggy runs into a brick wall called Boris Stankovich.

Isa halts the progress of Horacio Agulla.

Leading out the team against Toulouse in the semi-final at the Aviva.

Cian tries to find a way past Patricio Albacete and Yoann Maestri.

That hurts!

Rossy finds a gap, of sorts, between Census Johnston and Thierry Dusautoir.

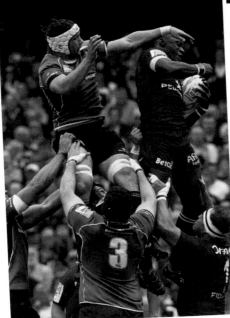

Kevin McLaughlin jumps against Yannick Nyanga.

Shaggy out-jumps Clement Poitrenaud for a spectacular catch.

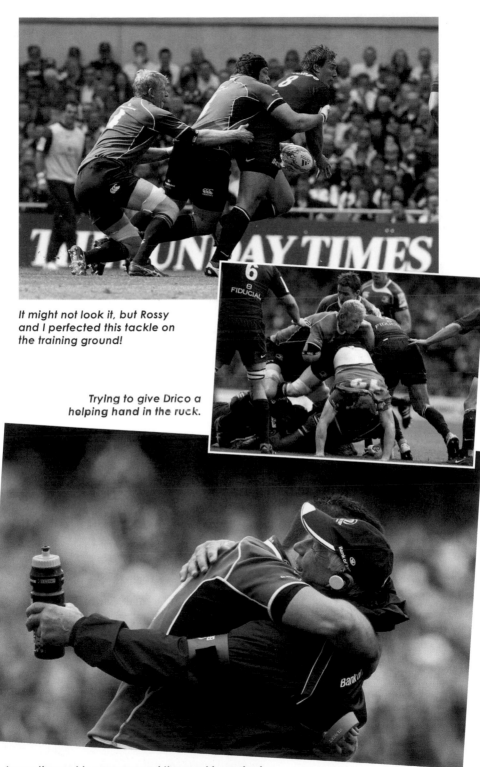

It might not look it, but Rossy and I perfected this tackle on the training ground!

Trying to give Drico a helping hand in the ruck.

Jonny throws his arms around the most important man in Leinster – our bag-man, Johnny O'Hagan.

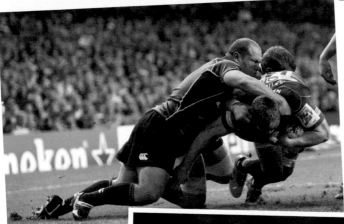

Another proud moment as I captain Leinster against Northampton in the final.

Straussy stops Chris Ashton just short of the line.

Shaggy runs into trouble.

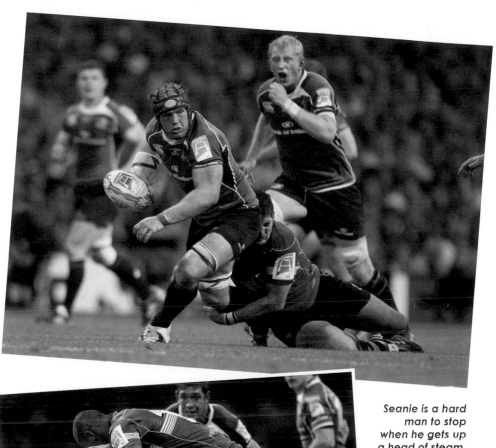

Seanie is a hard
man to stop
when he gets up
a head of steam.

Kev locks horns with
Courtney Lawes.

Drico weaves and jinks his way
through the Northampton lines.

Referee, Romain Poite, has a quiet word with me and Northampton skipper, Dylan Hartley.

Lukey proves he can tackle as well as run.

Jonny at his kicking best.

Jamie and I put an end to Roger Wilson's progress.

Darce makes it over the line but is held up.

Hinesy and Rossy try to slow down Soane Tonga'uiha.

Seanie carries on regardless.

Trying to avoid Paul Diggin.

Jenno gives Jonny a pat for making it across the line.

Drico and I hug at the end of a long campaign.

Drico and Jamie share a victorious embrace.

Lifting the cup!

Celebrating the win.

With Jenno.

With Jonny, Ferg and the Heineken Cup.

We've won – again!

Head of strength and conditioning, Jason Cowman, and I enjoy the victory.

We owe these guys a lot – Jono Gibbes, Joe and Greg Feek.

A great moment: sharing the success with my dad, Frank, in the Millennium Stadium.

Rehabilitation coach, Stevie Smith, myself and Kev celebrate.

The christening of my sister Sarah's son Fionn was a proud moment, which even 'over-shadowed' Leinster's second Heineken Cup success, for proud first-time grandparents, Frank and Paula Cullen. Though my mum has always been my greatest supporter!

The next generation? My sister Sarah fits her son Fionn into the Heineken Cup at Dublin airport.

The most important person in my life: my then-fiancée, Dairine Kennedy ... and the Heineken Cup!

My 'other' big day: marrying Dairine.

one of his testicles was left hanging outside his sac. Shelford also lost four teeth in the same incident, but he told the team physio to stitch him up. He then returned to the field and, shortly after that, a punch laid him out and he had to be taken off the field concussed.

There I was, thinking of Buck Shelford!

But, I also quickly rationalised that there was no comparison between a test match which the whole world seemed to be watching and a Magners League game in the RDS. It was no time to do a Buck Shelford. I was down on one knee, thinking all of this through.

When I was brought into the medical room and got stitched up, the burning began to ease but there was a huge discomfort in trying to move.

Or trying to walk.

All the lads had looked at me walking off the field and doing my best impression of a John Wayne walk. It did look like I had been sitting on a horse for three days, and they laughed when I came back out and joined the subs bench in the second half. Drico was there and he thought it was the funniest thing of the night.

He'd been 'water boy' with Jamie and, when they realised what had happened, they could not get back to the bench fast enough to tell everyone about it. By half time, everyone was talking about it. John Ryan, another one of the Leinster team docs, had the unenviable job of inserting twelve stitches into my scrotum.

I was still walking like John Wayne after the game, but I got some food into me in the dressing room and headed home.

I was given a special protective cup, which I wore when Ireland played Wales and England, and continued wearing for the following few weeks. I was able to get by just fine with that. Though, after the English game, I needed to get my scrotum re-stitched.

John Ryan was also on call at that match and when he inspected the wound it was like something from a horror movie. There seemed to be blood everywhere, and the pain was excruciating.

I have no problem in admitting that, as I moaned at him, and screeched a bit, I was no Buck Shelford.

When the referees were named for the Heineken Cup quarter-finals, we got Nigel Owens. Again. He'd been the man in the middle as we navigated our way to the final through the three knockout games in 2009. It was a good omen.

Teams spend as much time analysing the referee as they do their opponents, and it's amazing how they can differ in small ways. They all have their own trends and peculiarities, which are worth getting to know in advance.

We know Nigel extremely well, as he has officiated dozens of Magners League games as well as Heineken Cup games, and he's good. One of the very best. At the same time, he's different to Poite and Pearson.

My first game back with Leinster when the Six Nations had finally ended, was against the Dragons, in Rodney Parade in Newport, where we had sent a young team the year before and got absolutely thrashed. It turned into a bit of a dogfight.

But it was good being in a dogfight with Leinster. I'd missed playing with the lads and it felt great being back where I always feel I am supposed to be, I guess. Jonny, Redser and myself were back in action but Jamie, Seanie and Mike Ross were given another week to get themselves together after what had been a more gruelling Six Nations campaign for the three of them.

We beat the Dragons 26-16 to maintain our push in the League, but only after they blew a couple of good chances early on.

We got out of the place without suffering any injuries, which was good. The injury list in camp was actually very short for that time of year and guys were talking about the Heineken Cup more and more, and jockeying for positions. Six days after the Dragons, we had Munster in Thomond Park which was the ideal game to get everyone's minds right and also allow Joe and his coaching team to see who was coming into form at the right time of the season.

Shane Horgan was playing his 200th game for Leinster and Shaggy had the honour of leading the team out, and it was fitting that he should do so against Munster in their own backyard.

Shaggy had fought longer and harder than anyone still in our camp to make Leinster the No. 1 rugby team in Europe. He'd been there during the bad days.

Winning one Heineken Cup and targetting a second victory was everything he had ever wished for, and he was playing better than ever.

Shaggy is especially crucial for us in the bigger games. He is a real leader in the dressing room and I could not have been any prouder walking out behind him in Thomond Park.

Before we made our annual trip to Thomond Park at the beginning of April, we were in second place in the League with Ulster, 12 points behind Munster.

Our 24-23 defeat gave Munster a firm command at the top of the table, and had the League been run off as it was in the old days, and not had semi-finals and a grand final, then Munster would have been home and dry.

It was a very strange game.

We played well and looked very comfortable against them for long periods. We were 20-9 in front at half time, though, in truth, it should have been more. Our defence was very good and we were winning quick ball at the breakdown and causing them problems. Jonny kicked five goals in that first half. We also scored a wonderful try in that first half, which naturally came from the man of the moment, Shane Horgan. He crossed their line in the 21st minute. We were doing everything just right but, then, inexplicably, we seemed to drop our intensity completely.

It was like we quit on the game.

All of a sudden, we were getting bundled into touch. We were not making the tackles which we had made in the first half, and they began to assert themselves completely.

They still didn't score a try – our defence was that good – and, afterwards, it was very strange indeed to be told that we had outscored them ten tries to nil in the last six meetings between the two teams. So, how did we hand them the game? That question was on the mind of every Leinster player on the team coach on the journey home.

The main reason we lost was that we gave away cheap penalties and, with Ronan O'Gara kicking eight goals from nine attempts, that was complete madness on our part. The penalty count in the second half completely blew us off the park, all on its own.

When we went behind in the second half, we actually got our act together again and regained the lead. But it was short lived. We quickly gave away another dubious penalty for ROG to whack over from out on the sideline in the last minute of the game.

It was a bad second half, and it was a really sickening way in which to lose a game. I had a lot to think about on the coach ride home. In 2009, just a handful of weeks before we won our first Heineken Cup, we had been killed down in Thomond Park, 22-5, and, even though we missed with three or four handy kicks at goal, there was no hiding from the fact after the game that we still lacked real self-belief as a team.

At least we didn't have that problem any more! However, we did need to push ourselves more. I realised that. We needed to be harder on ourselves and expect more for the full 80 minutes of every game. At half time in Thomond, we had the opportunity to finish off a big performance.

But we lacked that killer instinct.

That worried me the whole trip home. I didn't mind losing to Munster. We'd had a good series of wins over them for a year or two, and I had never been counting up those wins in my head. The only thing that worried me, and annoyed me, was that we did not seem to have the instinct to finish teams off when we had them at our mercy.

By the time we finally came into Dublin, I had calmed a lot. I saw the benefits of losing the game, and the most significant benefit was that it had given every last person in our dressing room a good kick up the backside one week before we recommenced the Heineken Cup with our quarter-final against Leicester.

Leicester were coming back to the Aviva with five English players in their ranks who had suffered the massive disappointment of being unceremoniously turned over by Ireland in the final game of the Six Nations Championship.

They had that huge motivational weapon.

The other big advantage which Leicester held was their unique abilities in the lineout. They have the ability to get three men in the air from a seven-man lineout, which is something that is beyond the reach of most other teams. With three 'pods' they are tough to call against. Someone like Tom Croft, for instance, does not need two people lifting him. Normally, however, Newby jumps at the front for them with a one-man lift, while Croft, Louis Deacon and George Skivington move up and down the line. I knew I had to get my own personal homework exactly right for them.

They had also beaten Harlequins in the Premiership, the same weekend as we tumbled in Thomond Park. That left them with ten wins in eleven matches in England, so obviously they were bang in form.

But, it was more than form. Leicester, still, hold a massive psychological advantage over most other teams in England, because very few teams have the mental strength to stand up to Leicester.

They are classic bullies.

Impressive bullies! Every other team would like to be able to bully like they do, but it takes years and years of systems and structures within a club to produce a team with Leicester's mental toughness. Physically, too, they have so many big, powerful men who are able to run over opponents.

I admire them hugely, and everything they represent. For so many other top rugby teams, Leicester are still the team we would all like to emulate.

To beat them, I knew we had to manipulate them, move them around, stop their power game in its tracks. As a classic juggernaut team, they don't like having to restart the big engine all over the field.

I knew what to expect from them. I knew what they wanted to do to us. However, it is one thing having that knowledge and it is something else entirely doing something about it.

That is the big challenge, always, for every team which faces Leicester every single week.

The wait for the quarter-final had been too long.

We had been thinking about them, and talking about them, for too long, but that is how the Heineken Cup is structured and we just had to get along with it. Back in the week leading into our game against the Dragons, Joe had taken us down to Johnstown House in Enfield for a get-together for a couple of days, and we had spent one of those days talking about Leicester and only Leicester.

We set our goals at that mini-camp, and reaffirmed our targets for the remainder of the season. We had also other bits and pieces to do as well, like getting to grips with the issue of social media!

That had become a little bit of a problem for many teams, including us. The Irish squad had set down guidelines to all its players that they were not allowed to 'tweet' pre-game or post-game, for a period of 24 hours either side of the game. We decided to adopt a similar model in Leinster.

The Tuilagi brothers, Alex and Manu perfectly represent the power within the Leicester team better than anybody. You just have to look at them standing still to get a strong sense of what it is like to play a game of rugby against them. They are an amazing sight. Standing or running with the ball.

I played with Alex in Leicester and he was a naturally huge, physical specimen. He's 124 kilos, he's got speed to burn and once he's moving he is nearly impossible to stop. Manu is more of a young Englishman.

Manu is one of those perfect models of a modern rugby player, whereas Alex is more relaxed about life. He's never that worried about anything. When you are built like him, I suppose you don't need to be too worried. When people talk about genetics, they just need to look at the Tuilagi brothers. They have all the genes!

Since my days with Leicester, Richard Cockerill had become Head Coach at the club. It was easy for me to imagine how he was preparing his team for their visit to Dublin.

Cockers never gives anyone too much credit, for starters. It is hard earned with him. I knew he'd look closely at us, but tell Leicester that they were a better team than us. That's always his attitude.

"We're a better team than they are, and we're going out there to win...

End of story!" That's pretty much his No. 1 message to his players. I'd spent a lot of time with him in Leicester, as he was the forwards' coach at that time, and we had an up and down relationship. He's a tough task-master and a hard character, but he gives massive attention to detail and the basics of the game.

Nobody knows the Leicester way better than Cockers.

As a team, they never stop, not for a single minute, working on the basics of the game. And Cockers, expecially, wants his forwards working on basics, basics, basics all day long.

Repetition. Repetition. Repetition. That's the Leicester way, they literally belt the basics into players on the training field. Therefore, it would have been hard not to learn during my two seasons over there with them.

In Ireland, perhaps we look more at the overall nature of the game. That's the kind of game we play and so that's the way it is here. They're different. Leicester are the ultimate English rugby team.

Cockers is an ideal coach for them. I played against him a few times, earlier in my career, and he was the sort of bloke who would give you a box just to see how you would react.

Our Captain's Run in the Aviva on the Friday was very good. Everyone was sharp. The mood was close to perfect. However, there was also an edge and players were bouncing off one another just a little bit, which is also very good to see. That's what I wanted.

We were without Jenno and I realised that he would be a massive loss, not just in the game, but also in the 24 hours before the game. Jenno is a big talker for us. He's also, like me, a former Leicester man and therefore having him in the mix in the dressing room would have been an even bigger advantage for us in our preparation.

But, if we were without Jenno, they were without Geordie Murphy -and, I suppose, that evened things up somewhat. Geordie is one of the longest-serving players in Leicester and one of the soundest men I have ever played the game with. He's a class act on the rugby field, too. I was sorry for him, personally, but professionally it was a big help seeing them without one of their very best players. In big games, Geordie has that knack of presenting his full genius on the field.

His career path took him away from Leinster, and he was a loss. He's won everything in England and Europe with Leicester but, in Leinster, we missed out on a very special player.

Our rivalry with Leicester has grown slowly over the years. Before 2011, we'd played them ten times during my career, all in big games which people tend to remember. We had each won five of those games, going right back to 1996 when they came to Lansdowne Road and won 27-10. But, as clubs, our respective journeys over those years could not have been any different.

They have always been the model of consistency, whereas we were one of the most inconsistent teams in Europe over the same time period. However, we were always able to peak for games against teams like Leicester. We always had the ability to win the one-off game. But, we never had what Leicster had – an ability to win on the 'bad' days when we were not playing well.

Leicester are taught to grind it out, on good days, and bad days. Sometimes, it would be hard to distinguish between a Leicester performance on a bad day and their performance on a good day, and that is probably the ultimate compliment to any team.

Leinster on a good day versus a bad day? That's not worth thinking about!

Our biggest failing over the last ten or fifteen years was not doing it week in and week out. We always made such a huge emotional roller-coaster of so many seasons, which is something Leicester would never have experienced. If they win, it's no big deal in Welford Road. If they lose, it's still no big deal in Welford Road. They get on with life, either way, and get back down to the basics and get their next performance right.

They also have such outstanding structures and facilities in Welford Road. They have never left very much to chance and, in fact, they were one of the very first rugby teams in these parts to introduce a canteen system at their club so that they could closely monitor their players' food in-take.

Leicester is also such a community-based club, which was one of the things I loved most about being there.

As a rugby club, Leicester could not be further away from the bright lights of the big city. The Chairman of the club, for the last twenty years or so, is a gentleman by the name of Peter Tom, who also played for the club most of his adult life.

"We'll keep our arses close to the ground!" That was Peter Tom's favourite saying of all, and that's what he would advise us to do as players. Best advice there is, in my book.

When it came time for me to leave Leicester, I'll always remember sitting down with a couple of their officials. They wanted to know why I was leaving and, in truth, they could not fully understand my decision.

"You'll win nothing back there!"

That's what I was told, in so many words. They did not mean to be insulting at all. They wanted me to stay in Leicester.

We knew it would be an entirely different game to the Heineken Cup final of two years earlier. Besides, nobody in the Leinster camp cared to look back. We had a new coach and we had new players in, too. However, we were looking to snatch some motivational items from the past and some video clips were produced which showed Leicester trying their very best to intimidate us in old games.

It was more important to look at stuff like that in snatches of old games, rather than enjoying clips in which Leinster looked very good against Leicester. After all, we were taking on the classic schoolyard bully, and we could never allow ourselves to forget that.

Lots of big games sometimes boil down to the smallest, littlest things, and, in games like that, Leicester nearly always thrive. The simple things, done well, is sometimes the hardest task of all in big games.

Our preparation was all very routine. Leicester may have had the Leicester way, but in Leinster we had fallen into the Joe Schmidt way. It suited us perfectly. Everything was kept very light on the training field. It was all about freshness in the early days of the week.

Joe is hugely into keeping his pitch sessions to 60 minutes or less, and this is especially the case at the business end of the season. Monday was 40 minutes. Tuesday was 50 minutes. On Thursday we had 45 minutes, and that was it, really. It was all about the intensity, getting things right under pressure, and then leaving it at that and freshening up for the game. Lads were allowed to spend more time out of camp than normal, if that's what they wanted.

The Joe Schmidt way.

However, Nathan Hines, Kev McLaughlin and I spent more time in camp than anyone else that week and we spent most of that time working on our defensive lineout. It was time very well spent.

We stole a lot of ball from their lineout in our quarter-final victory. However, 24 hours before the game, I had never been as nervous in my life. I didn't know why. Perhaps it was because I had spent so much time during the Six Nations campaign not playing any rugby? Or, perhaps it was because, during that long period in the Six Nations, I realised just how important the Leinster team is in my life?

I was too wound up.

I stayed at home far too long that week and had foolishly locked myself away from all distractions. I became cooped up. I concentrated on the game for far too long. I spent far too much time doing my homework on the game.

Winning in the quarter-final, and beating Leicester, was more personal than ever before for me. And far more personal than the 2009 Heikenen Cup final had been for me.

They made all of the right noises the week of the game. They were utterly respectful of us and the Aviva Stadium. Cockers gave nothing away. He knew that he had a good hand to play, and he was keeping it as tightly against his chest as he had ever done.

Arses low!

There was no question of their five English boys coming to Dublin to avenge their 24-8 Six Nations defeat. Dan Cole, Louis Deacon, Tom Croft, Ben Youngs and Toby Flood were also keeping their arses as low to the ground as they possibly could.

But, there was no denying that Leicester were coming to win. They had such a head of steam. They had gone down to Harlequins, where they had turned around a 10-0 scoreline and edged out a 17-13 victory. That left them sitting strongly at the top of the Aviva Premiership table. They were looking to win the English title for the third year in a row. In attempting to do so, they had already scored the most tries in the Premiership (54 in 19 games), and conceded the fewest number of tries, and they had also scored 25 tries in their six Heineken Cup pool games.

Leicester had all of that.

And, of course, they had the little matter of their defeat by us in the 2009 Heineken Cup final at Murrayfield to feed off as well.

Cockers had an impressive hand of cards tightly against his chest.

We beat Leicester 17-10.

But, by the end of the game, we were hanging on. I would not have wanted the game to go on for another five minutes. To be honest, I would not have wanted another 60 seconds.

Another minute or two, and we might not have won. They had worn us down to virtually nothing. Granted, they were absolutely exhausted themselves, but, somehow, that juggernaut of theirs kept on coming at us, and coming at us.

I was absolutely and totally wrecked by the end.

I had to do a corporate appearance at a Volkswagen function in the stadium and I could hardly speak. I was finding it hard to stand as well, and ended up talking as I leaned against a wall to stop myself from falling over at any second.

I had never been more tired in my life. The truth, however, is that I was also tired before the game even started. I remember sitting in the dressing room and involuntarily yawning and then having to smother a second yawn a few seconds later.

My preparation had gone badly wrong.

I knew that I had been stuck at home for too long and had become far too anxious about the game, using up a whole lot of energy unnecessarily. I had not slept enough, either.

The adrenaline had kicked in a couple of days too early. I was over-hyped. There was no panic. I didn't feel that I was going to be in trouble or anything like that. I knew how to get on with it. But, as the game entered its last seconds, I also knew that I was just about out on my feet, and that if I had been in a boxing match one more jab on the chin would have had me down and out for the count. Having said that, everyone on the Leinster team looked out on their feet.

Another 60 seconds and we might have been gone.

At the beginning of the game, I sensed that we were a little bit off our game. It was like the Heineken Cup final in '09 in Murrayfield when both teams sort of shadow boxed during the opening stages. We were half creating chances, but not quite getting there. Then they started carrying and making yardage.

We were not totally flat but we were not right in that opening ten minutes. Some guys looked good and the scrum was strong. Our lineouts, too, looked to be in shape and, before the first half was completed, we had turned over five of their throws, which was a huge boost to us. We had some great reads, and Kev was superb. He was told to mark Tom Croft tightly and we knew that Croft would be thrown a lot of ball. I was marking Deacon to begin with and when he went off injured on the half-hour mark I had Slater to contend with, but that was okay.

Our dominance in the lineout starved them of possession and Leicester are a team who live or die by possession of the ball.

I was also happy to see Louis Deacon go! I admire the guy and have remained friendly with him since our Leicester days together. Like me, he was having trouble with his Achilles all season. He's the man who is at the very heart of their pack in so many ways, even though he does not say very much to anybody during the game itself. He's a tough guy, with no frills, and I knew it was going to be tough against him all day. Seeing him leave the field for good was definitely a good sight.

We created some great phases and, after one period of pressure, we had Straussy break their cover after Mike Ross had made some good yards, but the final pass to Lukey Fitzgerald just bounced unluckily off his chest. They were hanging in there. We led 9-3 at half time.

Jonny had kicked three smart penalties from three attempts, the first coming in the opening minute of the game when Isa Nacewa's kick infield was gathered by Lukey, and he sent me racing towards their line. They gave away the penalty. It was an excellent start, and so important to get first blood against them. Jonny's second kick had a touch of good fortune, as it deflected off both uprights before landing safely over the bar. His third penalty had come in the 36th minute after a brilliant run from Straussy. Toby Flood had kicked their first-half penalty.

We got everything from that first half we needed. The lineouts were brilliant and in the scrum Cian, Straussy and Mike were outstanding, with Cian battling to come out on top after having his hands full with Dan Cole early on.

There is always a key moment in games, and Leicester's appeared to come in the 43rd minute – they had a chance after they clattered into a ruck, and steamed over Jamie as he tried to place the ball. We were short on numbers defensively, after I came up and made a bad read and didn't stop the ball. Alex Tuilagi got the ball and he was off like a steam train. Drico went to tackle him.

Drico got run-over.

Alex ran straight over the top of Brian.

I remember looking down at Brian afterwards and he looked like he had just been run over by a train or a bus. His body looked crumpled. I had sympathy for him, because I'd been like that once.

One day, during training in Leicester, I tackled Alex while I was slightly off balance. At the time, I told people it did not feel like I'd been hit by a train or a bus. I remember clearly telling guys afterwards that Alex had felt like a high-powered BMW.

A phenomenal effort from Seanie O'Brien managed to prevent a certain try as Alex Tuilagi dived over in the corner. Seanie just knocked him into touch. He had the ball in his right arm, and his left arm just brushed the touch line. It was the break that Leicester knew they needed, but they didn't get that break. Nigel Owens went to the Television Match Official, Derek Bevan, for confirmation.

"Try or no try?" asked Owens.

Seanie duly got the decision of the TMO and his reward for his brave dive. The score would have left them 10-9 ahead and we would have been on the chase throughout the second half.

Our try must have taken their breath away, especially as it came four minutes later to double their disappointment.

It was that good, and Isa Nacewa could not have picked a bigger stage on which to showcase his incredible footwork and balance. He bamboozled half of their defence, after first gathering Youngs' kick near half-way, delivering the ball to Shaggy, taking the return pass, and then gliding his way around three attempted tackles.

But they came back at us. I knew they would. While Jonny missed the conversion to Isa's try, Leicester still could not get a foothold on the scoreboard and, two minutes after our score, Flood was badly astray with a very kickable penalty for them.

They started emptying their bench and began to really take the game to us with a vengeance. They had half-chances, and none better than when Slater spilled possession a couple of yards short of our line after Manu Tuilagi had run from deep.

Jonny increased our lead to 17-3 in the 75th minute but, out there, with them thundering at us, it never got to feel like a 14 points lead. All I could think of, during the last 20 minutes, was our defeat at Thomond Park, when we had let Munster off the hook and had suffered a bitter defeat as a result.

Losing hard-earned momentum in games is criminal. And not being able to break into a higher gear is the challenge for every team, and every individual, at the very top of their chosen sport. We lacked that gear against Munster, and also against Leicester.

They came back at us hard.

Leicester are the sort of team which can sense their opponents' frailties and self-doubts, and seeing us stop in our tracks like that had given them an even greater sense of hope and purpose.

When Flood missed one kickable penalty, I felt that they fell back a bit. But only for a few minutes. Then, they were hard at it once again. We had to keep tackling and tackling. Rob Hawkins had finally broken our defensive line and scored their try in the 77th minute and we had more tackling to do after that. Close to the end, as we held onto our 17-10 lead, I had a quick flash-back to a conversation I'd had with Joe earlier in the week, when we talked about the game going to extra-time if the sides were level at the finish of the 80 minutes.

And, I remember in that conversation, Joe emphasising to me that if it is still level after the extra-time then the winner is the team which scored the most tries. One more try from Leicester in normal time and they would have headed into extra-time with a 2-1 try count in their favour.

I could not get that chat out of my head in the final few minutes.

If they get one more try!

If they get one more try ... if they get one more!

If they crossed for another try then we would have had to get the decisive winning score in extra-time.

As the minutes counted down we were in a bit of a heap. We started to slip off tackles. They had effectively worn us down and left us like that.

We got there.

We survived, more than anything else.

We also deserved to win. We had some hugely influential individual displays, and none were more powerful and magnificent that Straussy's performance. He handed out, and shipped, more punishment than any other man on the field in either set of jerseys. We'd dominated them in the lineout, and in the breakdown exchanges and, most importantly, we had taken everything they threw at us and hardly flinched, until right at the very finish when we did look like a team which might fall over at any second.

I felt drained, from top to bottom, like a long bottle of someone's favourite drink. It was not just the 80 minutes against Leicester. It was the days waiting around, it was thinking about them, preparing for them every minute of every day all week long.

Cockers was really pissed off with the referee after the match and, being Cockers, he did not see why he should have to hide his complete displeasure with Nigel Owens.

I went home and got a couple of hours rest. But, at around midnight, I headed into the city centre.

The Leicester boys were having a blow out in town, in a nightclub, and I ended up joining them for a couple of hours, chatting with Geordie, Danny Hipkiss and Louis Deacon most of the time, but also having a few words with other lads I knew very well, like Castrogiovanni and Alex Tuilagi.

I was back in my bed by 3am, and out for the count.

Officially.

Heineken Cup
Quarter-final
Aviva Stadium, Dublin
April 9, 2011

Leinster 17, Leicester 10

HT: Leinster 9, Leicester 3
Attendance: 49,762
Man of the Match: Richardt Strauss
Referee: Nigel Owens (Wales)

—⁂—

Scoring sequence – 2 Mins: J Sexton pen 3-0; **4:** T Flood pen 3-3; **14:** J Sexton pen 6-3; **37:** J Sexton pen 9-3. **Half time 9-3. 48:** I Nacewa try 14-3; **75:** J Sexton pen 17-3; **77:** B Hawkins try, T Flood con 17-10.

Leinster: I Nacewa; S Horgan (F McFadden 75), B O'Driscoll, G D'Arcy, L Fitzgerald; J Sexton, E Reddan (I Boss 59); C Healy (H van der Merwe 78), R Strauss, M Ross, L Cullen Capt., N Hines, K McLaughlin (D Ryan 68), S O'Brien, J Heaslip.

Leicester: S Hamilton; H Agulla, M Tuilagi, A Allen, A Tuilagi; T Flood, B Youngs; B Stankovich (J White 75), G Chuter (R Hawkins 75), D Cole (M Castrogiovanni 52), L Deacon (E Slater 29), S Mafi, T Croft, C Newby Capt., J Crane (T Waldrom 62).

CHAPTER EIGHT

"NO GUTS, NO GLORY!"
Jamie Heaslip

Michael Cheika was entering his third season as Leinster coach when I came home from Leicester. There was still a good deal of work to be done, I thought. Cheiks had culled quite a number of players in his first year and he was still clearing his way through the system, and rebuilding the entire management organisation. He was doing a good job and was working as hard as he could with Mike Brewer as forwards' coach and David Knox as backs' coach

I was still delighted to be back.

It was also World Cup year. However, I was not really fighting for a place on the plane to France and had no expectations of getting the nod from Eddie O'Sullivan. When the phone call came from Eddie, at about 11.30 on a Saturday night, there was no great drama on this occasion. The conversation was business-like and I told him that I was expecting his call. I also told him that if there was anything I could do to help him and the squad, just to let me know.

I had been in Eddie's previous squad of 35 players but I knew that I was not in his sights. I watched the tournament unfold and, like the rest of the country, I was amazed to see the Irish team come apart as it did.

I really felt sorry for so many of the players I knew so well, and whom I had genuinely wished the very best in the tournament.

It was the storm before the end of Eddie O'Sullivan's career as Irish coach. He had done many great things with the team and their success in accumulating Triple Crowns will stand the test of time. I also thought Eddie was a very good coach.

In Leinster, with Brian O'Driscoll away on International duty, and a lot of the Leinster senior players with him, I deputised as captain at the beginning of the season. A great atmosphere had developed in the dressing room in a short period of time. Luke Fitzgerald was there. As was Jonny Sexton and Jamie Heaslip, so we had plenty of young talent in the team at that same time.

It was obvious to me that Cheiks was fanatical and hugely passionate about what he wanted to do with his team. The man was a ball of creativity and most of his ideas were excellent. Within weeks of coming home, I knew I had made the right decision to come and work for him.

I had brought with me my two years of experience with Leicester and, in the Leinster dressing room I had my own ideas, too. To begin with, I wanted to rebuild everything about the Leinster lineout.

The great thing about Michael Cheika was that, if he felt you were going to improve his team, he would open his arms to your ideas, he welcomed anything which would better his team. I talked with him and Brewer, and, in particular, sat down for a few chats about the lineout, as well as lots of other things about the team organisation.

"This will work." I told them. "Trust me."

And they did, which says an awful lot for Michael Cheika's and Mike Brewer's open-mindedness. Some coaches would not have wanted to know. Other coaches would not have been able to sit down with a player, without feeling vulnerable or undermined.

Not Cheiks!

The lineout went smoothly almost from day one, and the difference in the amount of ball we won – and the increase in ball we stole from our opponents – was there for everyone to see. There was also a solid pack of forwards in situ at that time, with Ollie le Roux, Bernard Jackman and Stan Wright in the front row, me, Mal and Trev Hogan in the second row, and Stephen Keogh, Jenno, Gleeson and Jamie working behind us at different times. It was not an ideal back row height-wise, but we worked our way through the 2007-08 season.

It was a hard season.

Drico suffered a lot of injuries. We played Munster down in Musgrave Park and he had to retire at half time. In the dressing room we regrouped and went out in the second half and found a real sense of unity of purpose. We had to have that in order to survive in Brian's absence. His absence forced others to bring the best out in themselves, and we did that that day and won.

Towards the end of that season, however, I damaged my shoulder again (for the first time since I'd had my surgery in October, 2003) and it was left completely unstable for the remainder of the season. I had a reconstruction job lined up for the end of the season and, by the time we won the Magners League, I had been in and out of hospital, and watched the final game from the sideline.

When I took over the team captaincy from Brian for the start of the 2008-09 season, I felt that, with three years of work completed, Cheiks had pretty much the squad of players he wanted. His fourth season held all sorts of possibilities. It had been great to be in England and win trophies, but I wanted to be part of a Leinster team which won the Heineken Cup.

Leinster still had a tag which identified us as underachievers. It was time to rip that tag off and force rugby supporters, and rugby teams all over Europe, to see us as a team which had grown into a whole new force on the field. To do that, however, we had to go out onto the field that same season and be forceful, muster our self-belief, and start winning 'big' games on the 'bad' days. That was the supreme motivation for me.

I wanted Leinster to win the next game and the next game after that, and become a winning team, like Leicester, and like Munster and Toulouse and the great teams I had been playing against for the twelve years of my adult career. I didn't have all the time in the world. I was thirty years old.

There was no more time for inconsistency. A winning mentality had to be with the team every single day. We needed consistency in our performance, and to do that we needed consistency in our preparation.

That's how it had worked for all of the great teams it had been my great honour to play against.

In my first year back with Leinster, we had been pooled with Toulouse, Leicester and Edinburgh in the pool stages of the Heineken Cup, and won three and lost three games in a disappointing campaign. Toulouse got the all-important away win, which helped their progress.

In the 2008-09 season, we had Wasps, Edinburgh and Castres to contend with in our pool, and we did enough to get through to the quarter-finals, but not enough to grab ourselves the advantage of a home draw.

But we got through our group, went to The Stoop – where we held out against all the odds against Harlequins and won in a ridiculously low score-line of 6-5 – then entered a packed stadium in Croke Park and finally defeated our greatest rivals, Munster, in an epic contest which we won by a *thoroughly impressive 25-6. We then finished the campaign with efficiency and massive composure in Murrayfield against Leicester, my second favourite rugby team, 19-16.*

We were crowned Heineken Cup champions.

Champions of all Europe.

It was an interesting season. For starters, it was a season in which we still met with good days and bad days and didn't always have our performance level up to the highest standard required. We had failed to get the four-try bonus point against Castres in the RDS and then we went to their ground a week later and self-destructed. I was injured and standing on the sideline watching that unfold in France, but I suffered as much as the players on the field.

We grew during that year and learned a little more about ourselves. By the end of the year, we knew how to prepare, and perform, as a winning team.

I was privileged to be Leinster captain.

I had seen Martin Corry break all the rules as Leicester captain.

After we had won the Premiership title with Leicester the season before, Corry had approached Jenno and me and asked the two of us to go up and accept the trophy on behalf of the team. As captain, he stood back, and let us do it.

At the time, I thought he was only asking me – since I had actually captained the team more often than he did in that Premiership campaign. But I quickly saw that he wanted Jenno with me, and that his decision had nothing to do with captains and vice-captains or anything like that. He just wanted the cup accepted by whoever best represented the spirit of the team at that particular time, and, as we were two Irishmen heading home, the Leicester captain felt that we should do the honours.

It was a humbling experience and a great lesson in my rugby life.

Chris Whitaker was one of my vice-captains that season and he was retiring from the game. More than anyone else, he had represented the spirit of Leinster that whole season and he was the natural choice to accept the trophy with me when the time came to step up onto the victory rostrum in Murrayfield.

We held the Heineken Cup together.

I can never remember seeing such colour at a rugby match. The two French quarter-finals in the Heineken Cup were magnificent to watch, and I sat back and took it all in. The occasions were a real feast to the eye, first of all the Catalan colours as Perpignan met Toulon in Barcelona, and then the Basque colours the next day as Biarritz and Toulouse went toe-to-toe in a brilliant match-up in San Sebastian which Toulouse won, 27-20 after extra-time. It was four French teams playing in two Spanish cities, with both grounds full to the rafters. It was an incredible sight.

Perpignan beat Toulon 29-25 in a real edge-of-the-seat match, and they earned themselves a semi-final against Northampton in Milton Keynes, which was sure to be a culture shock after the magnificence of the Olympic Stadium in their adopted city of Barcelona.

Northampton did not have it all their own way against Ulster. It was 23-13 at the finish, but Ulster looked more creative for long periods, and it was the Northampton pack which eventually won the day. Undoubtedly, Northampton have an excellent pack. Courtney Lawes was a bit of a human wrecking ball against Ulster, and Soane Tonga'uiha savaged their front row on his own.

We had Toulouse again in the semi-final, for the second year in a row. They had their shaky moments against Biarritz and, no doubt, Biarritz butchered a few chances which would have sealed the game for them. Dimitri Yachvili missed his kick from the touch line which would have given Biarritz the win, but it wasn't entirely the kicker's fault, because God only knows what Ilikena Bolakoro was thinking when he dived over in the corner for his try and didn't take his time in looking to touch the ball down nearer the posts and give Yachvili an easier conversion attempt.

While it was good to have the opportunity of avenging the 2010 semi-final defeat by Toulouse, I have to admit that I was plugging for Biarritz all afternoon. They would have been a safer bet for us. They have good players and they are a hardened team, but they are so up and down, and in the Aviva they would have been easier to turnover than Toulouse, there's no doubt about that.

On the other hand, with Toulouse, at least there was no danger of any complacency creeping up on us in our preparations. There were also some cracks evident in Guy Noves' team in their performance against Biarritz, and that was something to work on.

We had Ulster in the Magners League at the RDS the following Sunday, and they needed to put all of their eggs into the game and try to take something from a season which had looked very promising for them at different times.

But, with our unbeaten record at home, we were in no mood to go lightly on them just because they were out of the Heineken Cup. We are provincial rivals and big performances against Ulster have come quite naturally to Leinster in recent years.

We were in fourth place in the league table, three points behind Ulster who were second placed. We were in the last of the play-off spots, with the Cardiff Blues and the Scarlets hot on our heels, just four and five points behind us respectively. And after Ulster, we had two more games to make sure of, against Aironi away, and at home to Glasgow. It was a win or bust game for us, and we blew them away, even though the score-line was only 34-26 at the end.

We bagged the bonus point without delay, and had four tries on the board by the 36th minute, starting with Straussy who burrowed his way over the line after 60 seconds. Luke Fitzgerald, Shane Horgan (two) and Heinke van der Merwe scored the remainder of our five tries on the night. It was more of the same from us, however!

We talk all the time about putting teams away, and putting them away early, but when we build up a substantial lead we seem to back off.

I came off after 50 minutes, after clashing heads with Kev McLaughlin. I'd been trying to get my hands on Rory Best but met up with Kevin instead, but I was only left dazed and confused. There was no serious damage done.

The challenge, and the excitement, of the closing weeks of the season is what every player works for, and playing one of the great teams in world rugby in our home town in a Heineken Cup semi-final was exactly what we had wished for at the start of the season.

We didn't have a long and worrying injury list, but some players were out in the cold, nevertheless. That's the brutal, business-like nature of professional rugby. Rob Kearney's season had been effectively ended by injury many months previously, in November, and after having his left knee re-jigged with a cartilage refit he was left with a long, slow period in rehab.

Like everyone recovering from injury, Kearns was on a different programme to us, and in that sort of situation it is very easy for a player to feel something of an outcast. Though Kearns is one of the spirited, optimistic types who never appeared to have a long face on him at any time.

Dave Pearson was named as our ref for the Heineken Cup semi-final.

That gave us something to think about, and work on, as he had blown Ireland off the field against France in the Six Nations Championship. He was so tough on us, I thought, and he was especially harsh in his decisions at the breakdown.

We knew we would have to be extremely wary of that area against Toulouse, with Pearson watching us. Toulouse are a team who like quick ball, and Pearson is a referee who encourages quick ball.

At the same time, Pearson is one of the best referees on the circuit, and players have faith in him.

But, he is still a referee who suits a team which likes fast ball.

In the Stadio Luigi Zaffanella, in Viadana, we grabbed a 20-9 victory over Aironi and got out of town without any injury worries. That's all that we wanted from our quick trip to Italy. A win, the second placed spot in the league which that would bring, and a home draw in the Magners League semi-finals.

Most of all, nobody wanted to get injured, not with Toulouse around the corner in the Aviva. We did what we had to do in the first half, with

Seanie and Cian Healy grabbing a try each, and with Ferg McFadden kicking 10 points. It was game over at that point.

I was sitting on the bench and was happy to be sitting out the game. It was beautiful weather, very hot in the early part of the day and warm and balmy in the evening. Not really rugby weather. When we visit beautiful old cities in either the south of France or Italy, it's hard not to imagine what the flip-side of our careers would be like if we lived and played in a place like Viadana. I think the thought crosses everyone's mind in places like that.

But, not for long.

The day before we played Toulouse, I got out and about and I even met up with an old buddy, Ian McLaughlin, in a nice coffee shop and chatted about things for an hour or two.

There was no way I was going to make the same mistake I had made before the quarter-final against Leicester, when I'd been sitting at home for so long that I felt as energised as a family's pet budgie when the time came to head to the Aviva. For the semi-final, I relaxed more and actually thought about Toulouse less than I had thought about Leicester, which was some feat.

In camp there was, of course, some mention of 2010, when we left the Stade Municipal after a fairly demoralising 25-16 defeat. It was referenced here and there by different people, but it didn't need to be talked up to any great degree because that game was still in everyone's heads.

Besides, we were a different team in April 2011, to the Leinster team of April 2010, very different and, unlike the previous year, there was a much greater sense of expectation amongst our supporters, the media and rugby people, generally. It had been growing ever since the quarter-final and it led to a sizeable amount of pressure.

I could feel that pressure, but when I looked around me I wondered if the immediacy of the game, and the size of the game, was fully impacting on everyone in camp. Everyone was listening and taking it in, but, somehow, I felt that as a team we were not quite 'there' in the day or two before the game.

Toulouse had an impressive 33-0 win over Bourgoin the previous weekend, which had guaranteed them a home semi-final in the Top 14. Their flanker, Jean Bouilhou captained the team and he retained the captain's armband when Guy Noves named his starting 15 for the Heineken Cup semi-final. Their regular captain, Thierry Dusautoir, had been struggling with an injury and he was kept on the bench. Noves also decided upon Jean-Marc Doussain at scrum-half ahead of Nicolas Bezy, and Clement Poitrenaud was kept at inside centre along with Florian Fritz, which also left French International Yannick Jauzion on the bench.

Joe Schmidt knew all of the Toulouse players, pretty much as well as his former Clermont lads, because he had coached against them so often and studied them for so long. Toulouse are one of those teams which are always in the sights of other coaches. When a team has seventeen French Championships and four Heineken Cup wins, then they deserve to be studied. Also, in Guy Noves' eighteen years as Toulouse coach, he had led his team to six semi-final wins out of nine appearances.

Joe knew Noves, too.

He spoke about him to the media on the Thursday press conference, and surprised me at how happy he was to talk about his opposite number. He explained how Noves had his life balanced perfectly, and that when he was not winning games, he was fishing and hunting, and when he was not looking for something to eat, he was out on his bike. He said he's had long chats with Noves about life outside of rugby.

Guy Noves had walked out on Toulouse in 1989, on a point of principle, but returned as coach in 1993. He's a winning coach and Toulouse are a winning team with a huge budget which is just shy of €30million per year, which includes a Michelin star restaurant and a couple of shops, as well as a huge staff under Noves.

The depth and richness of their squad is envied, even in the big-spending French league, and for the 2011-12 season Toulouse had already signed up Wallabies and Waratahs scrum-half Luke Burgess, Auckland Blues and All Blacks out-half cum centre, Luke McAlister, in addition to Stade Francais out-half, Lionel Beauxis.

We got our timing all wrong.

We had never got it so wrong in my three years since returning home to Leinster. We rocked back into the dressing room in the Aviva, after our warm up had gone as smoothly as ever. We have everything timed, down to the very last second, for all of our games and that carefully planned routine had never let us down.

But, when we got into the dressing room we had to turn around and head right back out onto the field. There was no time to catch our breath, or get together for a team huddle. Some guys had no jerseys on. Others were in the toilets, and some others were milling around the place doing what guys do in the last few minutes of preparation.

We had to get right back out.

Toulouse, the officials, and the television cameras were waiting.

We had to go!

Everybody was flustered leaving the dressing room, and there was a state of shock and mild panic at getting our pre-match timing so badly arse-ways.

When David Skrela's penalty bounced back off the post, five minutes into the game, we didn't quite have our wits about us as a team, even at that point. The ball veered in to clip the outside of the right upright and, typically, Drico was more awake than anybody else, but the ball bounced wickedly over his head and straight into the hands of Florian Fritz who had the easiest try of his career.

Even if we had been alive and fully tuned, there would have been little we could have done about such a bizarre score. The ball actually bounced into the in-goal area, and then bounced back over Drico's head! It was a freak of a thing. At that stage we had already lost two of our own lineouts. Getting together under our own posts was not a bad place to be, in truth, because we needed to get our heads together and start playing.

The first lost lineout was a bad call by me and I was beaten by Nyanga. The second one was an over-throw by Straussy. Also, our first scrum was whistled back for a free kick to Toulouse. All of a sudden, we had no territory, and no ball, and we were 7-0 down. Coming together under the posts was a bit of a blessing in many ways, because we needed to talk, and do so calmly and purposefully.

We may have been flat and slightly disorganised at the beginning, but the atmosphere in the stadium was so good, and so special, that the whole team sucked it in in the middle of that first half. When the Aviva is at full throttle as a stadium, it is an amazing place. It creates an atmosphere, a mood, all of its own which can be infectious.

I had thought in the days before the game, that our guys were not scared enough of the semi-final, for some reason. A team needs some fear because a mixture of confidence and fear is exactly the right combination of ingredients to extract a 100 per cent performance from any team.

Even a tiny bit of happiness and contentedness is dangerous. The attitude: 'If twelve players turn up, then we'll be alright' is so destructive. If even one or two people have that thinking then the whole team performance can be knocked out of its stride. We'd been running around like headless chickens for those first few minutes of the game.

Jonny kicked a penalty after 10 minutes to help focus everyone even more. It came after our first lineout win and smooth handling which launched Darce in midfield before we got that penalty.

But we were still at sea that little bit.

The referee, as we knew full well he would be, was very harsh with us at the breakdown. We couldn't slow Toulouse down. We needed to stop them in their tracks, but they were moving the ball around and they were definitely in control of the game. Skrela dropped a goal for them to regain their seven points lead. Then, Jonny kicked his second penalty.

Our try came after we got a penalty advantage.

We picked and went with the ball a good few times, and finally, after 18 phases, Jamie made for the line to score, stretched out his hand through a forest of legs and bodies to touch the ball down, just about. However, Dave Pearson called the play back for the penalty!

I told him we needed him to go upstairs to the TMO.

He agreed.

The crowd went wild when Jamie's score was repeated on the big screens. They definitely thought it was a try, and the atmosphere in the stadium turned from being great, to being absolutely electric. That end of the ground in the Aviva is a place all of its own, and it's where Drico ran in his try against England as well.

That end, somehow, with all of the people in it, is just so loud and colourful and is in direct contrast to the opposite end of the ground which is so sparse. It's, like, double the volume of a normal end of a ground, for some reason.

The TMO, Graham Hughes confirmed the score.

We were in front. The whole team rose a few extra inches off the ground from that point in the game and we realised that this was a day when we would shake off Toulouse. When we had the ball in hand, we looked so dangerous.

Problem was, they also looked lethal when they had the ball in their hands. It was going to be one of those days.

In the final minutes of the half, we met with mixed luck. It looked like Doussain had scored a try for them, but Pearson brought the play back and gave Drico a yellow card for playing the ball in an offside position which, at the time, I thought was extremely tough on us. They kicked the penalty to level the game at 13-13 but, crucially, Jonny struck another three points for us just before the break when their Argentinian lock, Patricio Albacete, infringed and we went in at half time in the lead.

Jonny was having one of those days where he could have closed his eyes and kicked everything and, by the end of the afternoon, he would have eight kicks from eight for a massive 22 points haul.

We lost the lead just as fast.

Four minutes into the second half, Picamoles scored a try and Skrela kicked the conversion to put them back in front, 20-16. We had been under pressure from the first minute of the restart. Pearson awarded them a scrum after we carried the ball back into our own 22 from the restart and put the ball out on the full with a clearance. This left us defending a 5-metre lineout, which, in turn, led to a scrum.

The first scrum collapsed and, on the reset, they got a bit of an angle on us and Seanie O'Brien got blocked in. He was actually held by Nyanga, who duly received a back-hander from Seanie for what he had done. It was a natural reaction, but Seanie did slap him one, and Nyanga went down like a sack of potatoes in fine Hollywood style.

It was one classic dogfight from that point.

It was also breathtaking to watch and to play in. From David Skrela's restart, after Jonny had made it 20-19 with a penalty, possession changed hands nine times. Both sides tore into one another, and tried to tear one another apart using the full width of the pitch and every touch of genius which could be found.

From a scrum, play moved on for about three minutes, with possession changing hands on several occasions and, eventually, Cian Healy made a break up the sideline, barrelled through Heymans and raced away from Medard, before he was tackled by Picamoles. We knocked the ball on and they were awarded a scrum! We then lost Cian who was replaced by Heinke van der Merwe.

In the scrum which followed, we got the shove on, and got it on well, and Heinke drove through them. It was one of the biggest turning points in the whole damned game. As Heinke drove through, he sent the 130kilos of Census Johnston into the air and the referee gave us the penalty.

The stadium exploded with noise again.

Jonny looked at me.

"Kick to the corner?" he asked.

I was thinking we needed to be in the lead. It was definitely time to get our noses in front again, I thought.

Jonny was still thinking, *corner*!

Jonny and I have that relationship. Sometimes, all it takes is a look from either one of us, but, in the 56th minute of the semi-final, with Toulouse having worked so hard to take the lead after half time, another three points would be like a thump on the side of the head to them. I told Jonny to kick it.

I knew it was still a tough kick.

But, I knew Jonny would slot it, and he did, and we were 22-20 in front. Off the restart, we moved the ball wide and got back into attack mode straightaway with one of our planned moves.

I was delighted that we had that mindset, despite all that was going on around us, to step back into our pre-match preparation. It is not always easily done.

But we had the headspace to do just that, and it was good to go right back on the attack, rather than take the easy option and simply kick the ball back to them.

Straussy re-gathered the ball, after Lukey had kicked over the top. We got a scrum and, a whole pile of good phases later, we scored our second try which resulted in Drico and Ferg looking like two right head-cases in their celebrations. But, their reaction was spontaneous and showed how fired-up we had become during the course of the game, after such a flat and mixed up start.

Drico's try, as so often, was a match-winner – there are few players I would rather see with the ball 5 metres out!

Jonny kicked the conversion and we were nine points in front, 29-20, with 20 minutes still to go. The dogfight continued.

They hit back.

We gave away a cheap penalty.

It was 29-23.

There were five minutes left.

They were right back in the game and of all the teams in world rugby who can conjure up something magical in the dying minutes of a game, it is Toulouse. Dozens of times, we had all seen them do it. However, I felt much stronger than I had felt in the semi-final against Leicester with five minutes to go in that game. Then, my legs were cramping up. Everyone around me was under pressure. We had so little left against Leicester as the game crept into its final two minutes.

Against Toulouse, everyone felt stronger and fresher.

We got another penalty in the final minute of the game. There was enough time to kick a goal, but there was also enough time to take a lineout.

What if the ball hits the post?

Sometimes, it is better to go with a lineout in that situation, stuff the ball up your jumper, and kick the ball out of play after that. It was one of those decisions.

I knew Jonny would kick it over, and Jonny knew that he would kick it for another three points. I told him to give it a good whack.

"Kick it dead!"

Jonny kicked it true.

The game ended. I remember looking at the blue throughout the stadium, and those blue flags and blue jerseys never looked so blue. There was a magnificent blue filling the whole stadium.

I never felt so proud in my life.

It wasn't just beating Toulouse! It was like we had played two games, back-to-back, against two giants. Leicester and Toulouse are two of the greatest rugby clubs in the world, and they had stepped into our home, one after the other, and we had taken care of the two of them.

I felt a great sense of excitement.

Two of the greatest teams there has ever been. All of their great players. Their power, and their history. We had to take all of that on, and we did, and we stood strong, and everyone in blue on the field, and everyone in blue in the stands shared in the magnificence of being Leinster.

Jamie Heaslip chatted to the press with me after the game. He summed it up nicely, I thought, when he was asked if our performance was driven by a huge need to take revenge for our defeat by Toulouse twelve months earlier.

Jamie said that Toulouse just happened to be in the semi-final of a competition which we wanted to win.

"They played some amazing rugby," he replied. "And we didn't play our best, but ... no guts, no glory!"

We'd come a long way.

And we were standing in a place where nobody thought Leinster would ever be standing, with Leicester and Toulouse at our feet.

There's nothing better than being in a Heineken Cup final and sitting back to see who's going to make it through the other semi-final.

Northampton looked impressive.

But, Perpignan? It was hard to tell if they were up for it or not. They had a big front row, and their tight-head, Nicolas Mas, is one of the best operators in the world, but Perpignan got completely beaten up and thrown to one side by the Northampton pack. It was interesting to see.

Soane Tonga'uiha, Dylan Hartley and Brian Mujati looked to have massive strength, and Phil Dowson and Courtney Lawes worked with their front row hand-in-glove. Also, their confidence grew through the semi-final and looked like it could grow some more. I wondered, as the five of them looked unbreakable in the second half in Milton Keynes, what Mike Ross was thinking to himself.

I believed that we had a better team unit than Northampton and, man for man, we had greater experience and more quality than they had. However, Northampton have what Leicester have always had, and that is great basics.

I could see that in their semi-final victory. More than anything else, they had true power, and that is a crucial weapon for any rugby team, young or old. Northampton had that power, and I could see that they were also cocky and confident, and had ideas that they were ready to take on the world!

As I looked at them pummeling Perpignan and winning in the end by a fine 23-7, I did wonder how Northampton would react if they were to experience the same sort of power coming right back at them, in a high-pressure situation?

May 21 would have to tell the story.

On the Monday after the semi-final, Seanie was able to take a deep and relieving breath. He was not cited for his altercation with Yannick Nyanga just as Toulouse scored their second try, which resulted in the French player being replaced by Thierry Dusautoir. It was clear that Seanie had been illegally held as Picamoles got in for that try.

Sometimes, fair is fair in rugby.

The 50-hour citing window passed at 5.30pm, and there was no case to be heard.

It's never a good idea turning up at awards nights when the curtain has not been pulled on the season. Awards nights on the rugby calendar, like in soccer in England, come early however, and, on the Wednesday night, we all had to show solidarity with the Irish Rugby Union Players' Association in the Burlington Hotel, and try not to bask in any congratulations or even the slightest reflection of glory.

It was hard, especially when Leinster players were being shown scoring tries on big screens in the room. And also when one of our own, Isa Nacewa became the first overseas player to win the (deep breath here!) Bord Gais Energy Irish Rugby Union Players Association Players' Player of the Year award.

It was an outstanding honour for Isa, and one which was totally deserved. Richardt Strauss won the Unsung Hero Award, while Mal O'Kelly was back with us for the night and was inducted into the IRUPA Hall of Fame.

The week after the Heineken Cup final, Sean O'Brien won the European Player of the Year, which was a fantastic acknowledgment of Seanie's magnificent season.

By the end of the Heineken Cup, Seanie had more carries (115) than any other player, as well as more metres than any other forward in the competition.

It was a busy week. On the Friday, we hosted Glasgow in the Magners League in a must-win for us, if we were to clinch a home advantage in the semi-finals. Jamie captained the team.

I sat it out injured.

Against Toulouse, I'd been absolutely blessed not to do serious damage to my knee when it got caught in the turf in one of the first lineouts and I went down in a bit of a heap. I thought I was going to have to go off. My leg got caught under me as I turned and I damaged my medial ligament. The next morning, in Santry Sports Clinic, I got the news that I had only suffered a grade one strain. I was a lucky man.

We beat Glasgow 38-3, and really put them to the sword in the second half when, I am proud to say, I also played my part. Even from the sideline, in my tracksuit, I had a miraculous hand in the game!

Actually, I was meeting a friend of mine earlier in the day for a bite of lunch in Roly's Cafe in Ballsbridge and I parked in Herbert Park, as usual.

As I was getting out of my car I spotted some rugby players running through a few things and I quickly recognised one or two of them, and jumped back into my car right away. For the next two minutes I had a good look at the Glasgow pack running through their lineouts. Later on, the information was dispatched to Jamie and Co.

We had the Magners League semi-final against Ulster to negotiate before completely getting our heads into the Heineken Cup final in the Millennium Stadium. The Ospreys headed over to Thomond Park the same weekend to meet Munster in the second semi-final, where they were beaten 18-11.

The Ulster game was Brian O'Driscoll's 150th appearance for Leinster, and Joe was not of a mind to put out a weakened team, despite getting the better of Ulster on more than one occasion earlier in the season. It was a courageous call. Joe likes momentum and he saw no reason to interrupt the team's settled look.

He also thought that Ulster would be a dangerous game for us. They had won eight of their previous nine League matches, their only defeat being to us in the RDS three weeks earlier when they were three tries down in no time.

We beat Ulster 18-3.

But, nobody celebrated.

It looked a very costly win. Afterwards, when we sat in front of the journalists, Joe called it a "demolition derby" and I'm sure they have the same "demolition derbys" in New Zealand as we have on this side of the world! Drico and Straussy were Joe's biggest concerns.

Drico injured his knee and did not return for the second half. Also in the medical room were Straussy (hip), Isaac Boss (hamstring), Mike Ross (shoulder) and Cian Healy (thigh).

Quite a full medical room. I hobbled around the pitch myself because I wanted to test my knee in a real contest to reassure myself that my knee was not worth worrying over. I got through it okay.

My only consolation, when I looked at our troubled medical room, was that Northampton had gone to Welford Road that same weekend to try to win their way through to the Premiership final, and had gone down 11-3 to Leicester. They hadn't reported any worrying injuries after it, but I guessed that the Tigers had left them sore and beaten up and had left them in two-minds about their own physical prowess.

That's what Leicester do.

We had reached the Magners League final. And, another epic contest with Munster was on the cards, but, first of all, we had a second Heineken Cup to win.

Heineken Cup
Semi-final
Aviva Stadium, Dublin
April 30, 2011

Leinster 32, Toulouse 23

HT: Leinster 16, Toulouse 13
Attendance: 50,073
Man of the Match: Jamie Heaslip
Referee: Dave Pearson (England)

—⁓—

Scoring sequence – 5 Mins: Fritz try, Skrela con 0-7; **10:** Sexton pen 3-7; **12:** Skrela dg 3-10; **15:** Sexton pen 6-10; **30:** Heaslip try, Sexton con 13-10; **38:** Skrela pen 13-13; **40 (+2):** Sexton pen 16-13 **Half time 16-13. 44:** Picamoles try, Skrela con 16-20; **49:** Sexton pen 19-20; **55:** Sexton pen 22-20; **59:** O'Driscoll try, Sexton con 29-20; **75:** Bezy pen 29-23; **81:** Sexton pen 32-23.

Leinster: I Nacewa; S Horgan, B O'Driscoll, G D'Arcy, L Fitzgerald (F McFadden 57); J Sexton, E Reddan (I Boss 53); C Healy (H van der Merwe 53), R Strauss, M Ross (S Wright 74), L Cullen Capt., N Hines, K McLaughlin (S Jennings 53), S O'Brien, J Heaslip.

Leicester: C Heymans; V Clerc, F Fritz (Y Jauzion 61), C Poitrenaud; M Medard; D Skrela (N Bezy 68), J-M Doussain; J-B Poux (D Human 46), W Servat (V Lacombe 78), C Johnston (J Falefa 68), Y Maestri (G Lamboley 61), P Albacete, J Bouilhou Capt., Y Nyanga (T Dusautoir 46), L Picamoles (S Sowerby 65).

CHAPTER NINE

"THIS WILL BE REMEMBERED ... FOREVER."
Jonny Sexton

I shake hands with everybody in the dressing room.

With a game just two hours away, the hand-shake is longer and firmer than normal, and with the nervous energy and sense of anticipation before every game, that hand-shake also makes me feel stronger.

I drop my kit bag on the ground, and head out onto the field. I check the conditions for the coin toss in mind. I walk around the field, and mentally map out the lineouts and what calls I will make in different parts of the field.

I walk up one sideline. And then the other sideline. I remind myself of what we will do in each area of the field.

Which call here?

Which call here?

Which call here?

That morning, I'll also have gone through my lineout options on the field, on a sheet of paper. I might have five formations going into a game. Each formation might have five calls. Maybe more. It depends on who we are playing and what we want to do in the match.

The lineout is a game of bluff a lot of the time. I've analysed the other team. They have analysed us. We each know one another's traits, one another's trends, one another's habits. As best we can, at least.

I like to spend this time, pre-game, on my own as much as possible. The only people I need to talk to, at that time before the game, are Joe Schmidt and Jono Gibbes.

I go back into the dressing room, and get my ankles strapped. I have my wrists taped, and I have some lineout calls written on the tape, though I rarely use those reminders. For starters, if it is wet, the writing gets smudged within minutes. It's just a process I use, and sometimes it helps to jog my memory.

I tape my fingers.

With one hour or so to go, Joe will come into the dressing room and spend maybe five minutes with the team.

When we're in the RDS, the forwards do some walkthroughs on the lineouts in one of the halls. Mike Ross, our scrum leader, will talk through different aspects of the scrum. Greg Feek will talk. Jono will talk. Myself and Jenno will talk.

All of us then begin our personal individual preparation. There's 40 minutes to go to game time. Some people talk. Most guys have their head phones on. I like to use head-phones when I walk around the field.

With them on, I can walk around the field and concentrate, and not talk to anyone. Sometimes I have the ear-phones in place, but don't have any music on at all. It's a message to people to stay away. And, I'm not one for getting into chit-chats before a game, with anyone, apart from chatting to Joe and Jono.

I'm always trying to get a feeling for the room, and assess the mood. That's a big thing for me. How does the place feel? Is the mood exactly right, or a little bit off? That balance is important.

When the balance is exactly right, the last 40 minutes in the room is easy. I don't need to say anything, or ask anyone else to say anything. When guys are not quite right, then it's a tougher job, working the room and making sure that everyone is good.

It's absolutely important to let everyone in the room know that we are not quite 'there' yet! That's what we always say!

Are we 'there'?

Where 'there' is, nobody knows.

It's just something we all feel.

With 30 minutes to go, I leave the dressing room. I run towards the field, and immediately turn to my right. Always to my right. I reach the halfway line (if we are playing in the RDS), and run straight across the field, and down the far touchline. I stop under the posts, and start some stretching. If there are too many kids or too big a crowd behind the posts, I move further infield.

The tackle bags are out, and I get in a few hits on either shoulder. I get a couple of lifts. The hookers do a few throws. We practise a few receptions. Then, it's into a huddle. People talk.

Jenno will always say something. He always talks. Drico usually talks. I might say something but, generally, I prefer to leave the talking to Jenno at that time. If we need to hear another voice, I invite somebody else to say something.

We do a half-lap. Start on the halfway and go around to the far corner, jog back in, and a drill is prepared for us and waiting. We break into forwards and backs. After that we throw half a dozen lineouts, which might include one drive. We hit some scrum set-ups. We huddle in.

Jono talks.

Some of the other forwards might also talk, but hot air can start to come out of lads' mouths at this stage as the final minutes start boiling towards kick-off. We get back into a team unit, and do some continuity drills. Four or five times we hit contact and clear over rucks.

We go to the far side of the field, and do a defensive drill. We hit the bags. Do one play off a lineout, and run the way we will play in the first period. Do just the one, and then it's back into the dressing room. We've got four or five minutes.

Joe talks.

Then Joe goes. Everybody has something last-minute to do. Toilets. Tightening boot laces. Fidgeting for the sake of fidgeting.

If I think we need to huddle, we'll huddle. If I think we don't need to do so, then we don't huddle.

It's game time.

I will have something, one last message in my head for the team. I might say that something. Or I might not.

At that stage, I know!

I know whether we are 'there' or not.

I was waiting for Northampton.

We'd all been waiting for them for weeks, since our nine points victory over Toulouse at the Aviva, but on this occasion I was actually waiting for them all on my own.

I was sitting on the grass at one end of the Millennium Stadium, with

Leinster's manager, Guy Easterby and our PR man, Peter Breen.

Our Captain's Run had ended fifteen minutes earlier, and the lads had all gone back to our hotel, the Vale of Glamorgan, which is about twenty minutes outside of the city. We had a one hour slot in the stadium, from 3pm to 4pm.

Then, it was Northampton's turn!

The ERC guys kept coming up to me and apologising.

"They're five minutes away," each of the ERC guys would chime. "We promise ... they'll be here in five!"

This was the second such promise I had heard from them.

It was better sitting down on the grass than standing. It was bloody hot in the ground, even with the place completely empty.

Such a fuss over that bloody roof!

In the Leinster camp, we actually didn't give a damn if they opened it or closed it, but the reporters had made a pretty big deal of it, and I knew people were talking about it, inside out. If we had a preference, we'd probably have liked to have it open. If the roof is closed then there's more of a chance of the ball getting that little bit greasy in the heat, and that can affect the skill level of a game.

Anyhow, the forecast was for blue skies and good weather – so why would anyone want to close the roof? Whatever! It was never going to be our decision, open or closed. That was down to the ERC and the ERC only.

That Friday afternoon, however, the ERC were not worried about the roof. Their only concern was that the Leinster captain would 'disappear' on them, and that the traditional photograph of the two rival captains (Dylan Hartley and myself, in this instance) coming face-to-face on an empty field would not be sent out to the world's media 24 hours before Saturday's 5pm kick-off.

"They say they are only five minutes away ... honestly ... just got caught up in some traffic since they last called."

The ERC man was now red in the face.

I was still sitting on the grass, now sipping from my bottle of water, doing a little stretching, for about twenty-five minutes.

"Five minutes... Honestly!" promised one of them, with his hand over his heart.

Everyone was flustered, but I felt okay.

I'd taken the journey from the English midlands to Cardiff before, and it's always a longer trip than you think it's going to be. With Leicester, who are neighbours and rivals of Northampton, we'd nearly always arrive down in Wales later than we wanted.

Ten minutes had quickly passed since the last 'five minute' promise.

Guy wondered what I wanted to do?

"We're staying!" I replied.

I kept telling myself to stay calm.

'If this is all that's going to go wrong this weekend, then there's going to be nothing to worry about!' I told myself.

"Relax ... they'll be here in ... five minutes!" I laughed.

Northampton arrived forty minutes late and, to be fair to them, their management and officials were as panicked and as apologetic as the ERC officials. But, their players then started shipping out onto the field. They were only in the ground for a walkabout, because they'd done their Captain's Run on their home ground before setting off on the motorway.

As they all came out of the tunnel, in ones and twos, I was there waiting for them. I was with the ERC photographer and we were waiting for Dylan Hartley, but I had to say something to them.

"How'ya lads...

... how's it goin'...

"How'ya lads...!

"How'ya lads...

... How's it goin'!"

It was a surprise to most of them to find me, the Leinster captain, at the end of the tunnel, all kitted out, tracksuit off, thighs taped, ready and waiting for them! Finally, Hartley and I made it to the middle of the field, shook hands, posed for a minute or two ... standing up ... down on one knee ... and then we shook hands again.

And... I was gone.

I just wanted to get back to the hotel to be with the team, but late afternoon traffic in Cardiff was now more like early evening traffic, and nothing was moving. Our bag-man and organiser of all things to all players, Johnny O'Hagan was driving. Guy Easterby and I were in the front of Johnny's van.

I was all kitted out in blue without my tracksuit, 24 hours too early and, no doubt, looking a strange sight to the people of Cardiff walking by and looking in. Already, I could see lots of Irish reg cars, with Leinster flags flying, around the city.

We thought we knew all we needed to know about Northampton. They'd shown their full hand, twice in Thomond Park in interesting Heineken Cup battles the previous season. They brought Ulster down in their quarter-final, and three weeks earlier they had made light enough work of Perpignan.

That semi-final victory was, really, mostly about Soanc Tonga'uiha, Dylan Hartley and Brian Mujati in their front row.

They had developed as a team in the twelve months since losing twice to Munster, and they were still evolving but, importantly, to us anyhow, Northampton had not arrived at a point where anybody knew how they would perform under the ultimate pressure. And that was where we had to make sure they found themselves in the 2011 Heineken Cup final!

The week before the Heineken Cup final, they were in Welford Road, and even though they only lost 11-3 in the end in the Premiership semi-final, they were actually bashed up by Leicester. I was delighted that they got through to play at Welford Road. I wanted them to experience Leicester before the Heineken Cup final, and I knew they'd be in a rough state at the end of it.

I watched that game over and over again at home.

I loved it!

Actually, I couldn't lose watching it!

If they had actually beaten Leicester, I'd have been just as happy, because it would have made Northampton a supremely confident bunch of lads – and, in addition, it would have reminded everyone in our camp that Northampton were the real deal, after all.

We'd played Ulster in the Magners League semi-final in the RDS the day before that Leicester-Northampton game and, with 10 or 15 minutes to go, we were in a position where Joe Schmidt could afford to take some of our lads off the field. There's a huge difference between playing 60 minutes at the RDS (which was the case for most of us – those of us still on the field, and those who had departed!) and playing a full 80 minutes at Welford Road. Against Leicester, Northampton found themselves in a thorough, 100 per cent attritional battle, and they had no escape until the final whistle was blown by the referee.

I could still remember how physically and mentally draining our quarter-final had been against Leicester – when we had the 'honour' of playing them in the Aviva, and avoiding one of the toughest rugby grounds in the Northern Hemisphere. In Welford Road, opponents have to stop a juggernaut.

Except, the juggernaut never actually slows down, or stops.

In Welford Road, Leicester hold onto the ball forever, and they keep going through the phases, and they make you tackle and tackle … and tackle. For most of that game, Northampton stood up to Leicester quite well, but near the end of a season in which they have relied on their frontline players too heavily, Welford Road surely cost them. During the Six Nations, when five or six of their bigger names had been on England duty, they showed that they didn't have the strength in depth they needed, and they lost as many games in the Premiership as they played during that period of time.

Northampton had already lost Tom Wood. He'd been massive in their back row all year, and he had been the best player in the Premiership and his loss, technically, made our job that little bit easier. It's the small things, the smallest margins in each game which make all the difference.

Northampton, still, had plenty of guys for us to worry about. They also had a confidence which, it seems, only young rugby players in England have!

Two of the Northampton lads are, of course, 'our lads' – Jimmy Downey and Roger Wilson. They are both very steady performers. I've got huge admiration for Downey. He left Leinster so long ago and moved through several clubs to get himself where he is now, at the very top of his game. I think he's proven that you should never give up on your dreams. Roger is also the model of consistency and is a key member of the team since he joined from Ulster.

They lost Wood, even though he'd been sleeping in an oxygen tent for weeks to try and fast-pace the hairline fracture in his leg. They had Wood out, but we had Drico coming back in.

That was actually a big swing to us.

Brian limped off against Ulster after injuring his knee, but he was never in any real doubt of missing the final even though our camp continued to play out the line that he might be in trouble. We knew he would overcome his injury and get himself onto the field, whether he was 90 per cent fit or 100 per cent fit.

That's Brian!

Actually, Brian O'Driscoll is a wonder to me.

In the last ten years I've tried to figure out the Brian O'Driscoll who has become one of the greatest Irish players of all time, and one of the few 'superstars' of rugby on the world stage, but I can't. I've often wanted to ask him, occasionally, how it happens for him.

Or how he makes it happen all the time.

But how do you bring that up in conversation with a team-mate without looking like a total pot-hole?

Incredibly, he has this innate belief, which grows, every time he gets onto a big stage. He wants to be there. He wants to be his best out there. But, even on the training ground with Leinster, he amazes me with his crazy, fired-up competitive instinct which never, ever dims. I'll never understand how somebody can have that!

But now, with Leinster, Drico and I, and some of the older lads, do have one massive characteristic in common, and that's an unyielding desire to prove to people, over and over, and over again, that we will never again be under-achievers.

Personally, those days will grate with me forever.

I was so nervous those last few days.

It never works for me when I hear people say "You're older ... you're coming to the end of your career ... enjoy it."

If only life was like that.

Besides, I don't want to think like that. I'm not counting down the last days of my career. I'll leave that to other people who actually make these decisions.

I was so nervous because the final meant so much to me. It meant so much to everyone. You could see it all around the place. You had people talk to you on the street. You could see it in local businesses. You could see it with the flags on cars. You knew how people felt, and that brought a responsibility which can never be taken lightly.

And then there's family and friends ... and their excitement.

My parents, Frank and Paula, were travelling. My brother, Owen, was travelling. Dairine and her parents were travelling. A heap of my best friends were travelling.

The week was huge.

Why wouldn't I be bloody nervous? When you are captain, you happen to think about everything.

How's the mood in camp?

How's he feeling ... and what's he thinking?

Will I say something?

What am I going to say?

Is it the right time to say anything?

On top of that, we had been 'flat' for most of the week.

I sensed it.

Maybe it was natural to be like that when we had come through Leicester and Toulouse, and we had won all the big games and all the small games, and believed we were almost there.

A team can get into a routine and get a little bit complacent.

It's a natural reaction.

You truck along winning games, with people patting you on the back and telling you how good you are, until you get a mighty big shock!

There was definitely a little bit of that going on. We were

trucking along. Everything looked comfortable. But, there was massive danger ahead.

Where?

There was the danger that people had been paying lip-service and had not been taking the key messages on board, and it's only when you get into that position, the position of being found out, that you actually realise that you have dropped down a gear sometime before.

We had been trucking along okay in training and in team meetings, but the buzz had died a little, ever so slightly. The problem was that the coaches and the fitness staff were hugely into keeping everything fresh and sharp in everything we did at that late stage of the season, but with such sharp sessions we had less time to do things that we might have wanted to do, or talk through things which we might have wanted to talk through.

And, naturally, because we were coming to the Heineken Cup final, and the final two games of the season, everyone had loads of ideas!

"Why don't we do this?"

"What about that?"

"This?"

"That?"

"This?"

It was hard to squeeze everything in.

It's good to hear the others talk, and the passion and desire is fantastic when lads talk. But, as a result, things which should be done, or said, are sometimes left to one side.

All of this was in my head and had been there all week.

It was a different pressure, and certainly a different nervousness, to 2009. We didn't know what to expect coming into the final in '09. We'd never been in a European Cup final before, and we had no idea what winning would feel like?

Back then, there was also a sense of desperation within the team, and that had been there for a while, building itself up, because we had worked so hard on the mental side of our game for so long, under Cheiks, and also with Enda McNulty, and we had scraped through against Harlequins, and then it all came out against Munster in that semi-final in Croke Park on that incredible day in our lives.

We got our tries either side of half time. Rocky made his big runs. It was a day when almost all of the moves we had planned all year long worked out ... perfectly!

Drico got his intercept try, and we were out of sight.

All we had to do was tackle for the rest of the game! They were turning down shots at goal, and going for the corners, and we just had to defend and defend.

Leicester had won the Premiership the week before the 2009 Heineken Cup final. Thank God! I was praying they'd beat London-Irish, even if it meant Bob would lose out on his biggest reward of all. In that final we wanted it more than them. We were absolutely desperate to win!

'THE TEAM THAT WANTS IT MORE WILL WIN!'

Posters with those words were plastered all over our dressing room walls and on the walls in camp, and as it turned out we played only okay in the final, but we won because, simply, we wanted to win more than Leicester.

Amazingly!

Pure desire to win was the single difference between the two teams in Murrayfield that afternoon. We were also lucky, I suppose, that Leicester did not turn up for the first half! They got into their stride coming up to half time, but by the end of the game they were exhausted.

Waiting for the 2011 Heineken Cup final, however, we knew what it is like to win, and we were hot favourites to win. But, without the fullest desire ... would we win?

Like Leicester in 2009, we had the pedigree in 2011 and Northampton were the unproven team, and I kept wondering how great a desire would Northampton have when they got out on that field.

They had won all six games in their pool – and a team which wins all three games on the road in their pool must have some real steel to them.

I kept thinking that we didn't know enough about Northampton, but I also believed they had more to find out about themselves as well.

It made them dangerous.

It made me nervous.

They had not played a team like Clermont or Leicester or Toulouse in Europe during the season, and they had not played a team like us. They beat Ulster in the quarter-final, but we had beaten Ulster comfortably three times. And they beat Perpignan in the semi-final, but Perpignan don't travel well normally, although they had got themselves a draw in Welford Road in the pool stages.

We didn't know for sure what Northampton were made of.

So many people had said, in the last few weeks before the final, that it takes a great team to win the Heineken Cup once, but that if Leinster won it twice in such a short period of time, that it would tell a whole different story about our team.

I liked that pressure.

I liked the nervousness, too, and I liked the fear we had of possibly having to stand out there on the field at the end of the game and watch Northampton lifting the trophy... Watching Dylan Hartley lifting up the Heineken Cup... People laughing at us... After all the great wins and wasted work... People telling each other that we took Northampton for granted... Telling us that we did not give Northampton enough respect!

That was filling my head as well.

I was one of the few Leinster players who had ever played against them. With the Tigers, I played against Northampton four times in the Premiership, and they were all big games.

Massive games between two neighbours.

The first time, in Welford Road, in my first competitive start, it was a game that our lads were fired up for, and we beat them comfortably and won a bonus point for ourselves. When we played them away that year, we won again – and it was actually one of the best performances I had in the Leicester colours in my two years in England.

We played them away at the start of my second year, and we won. But, then we played them back in Welford Road, at a time when we were top of the Premiership, and they were at the bottom of the table.

I was Leicester captain that afternoon.

We lost.

It was the only Premiership game we lost at Welford Road in my time there.

I thought my world had come to an end after that game, even though Leicester were still at the top of the Premiership table. It was a weird, difficult game. That home record meant so much to me and I felt that I had allowed something sacred to be broken that same afternoon.

I felt a massive responsibility for that defeat. Even though, looking back on it now, I can still see our kickers rushing three or four shots in front of goal and missing them.

What could I do about those kicks?

Nothing.

But, that answer didn't help me.

We'd lost to Northampton, and we'd lost to Northampton, of all teams, at Welford Road!

They had been in our half of the field, once in the second half only, when they scored a breakaway try – the guy ran it 'home' down the touchline.

We still could not put them away.

That was four years earlier. A lot of their team were only kids back then. They didn't know about it and everyone else had forgotten.

But it still mattered to me.

On the Friday evening, we watched Stade Francais – and we watched Cheiks bringing his new team to the point of victory in Europe.

Stade were beaten by one agonising point, 18-19, by Conor O'Shea's Harlequins in the Amlin Cup final, and that meant Cheiks needed Northampton to beat us the following afternoon if they were to qualify for the Heineken Cup the following season.

As usual, Mike Ross, who is our self-appointed Entertainments Officer set up a big screen in the team room so that we could all watch the game together, if we wanted to – those of us who were getting some treatment on the tables from the physios and those of us who were, simply, bored of hanging around the hotel.

Every time the camera zoomed in on Cheiks' face, everyone in the room tried out their best Michael Cheika impersonations. So, when Gonzalo Camacho went in for Harlequins' late try, and then Nick Evans kicked over the conversion from the touchline, there must have been seven or eight 'Michael Cheikas' in the Leinster team room shouting and roaring about the injustice of it all.

I had my own room in the hotel.

It was quiet in the room, which is good and bad.

Good, in that I was able to get through a big chunk of the book I was reading, Floyd Landis' autobiography *Positively False*. It's an interesting perspective by the American, who won the Tour de France in 2006, on being labelled a cheat within his sport. Of course, he also explains his innocence!

Being in the room, alone, also gave me quality time to go through our game sheet and my own team notes. At the end of the season, I tend to pick up those sheets more and more often in the last 24 hours before kick-off. You want to have all the detail off by heart.

You want to be thinking that detail all of the time, because in a game as big as a Heineken Cup final it is possible to be over-powered by the day itself, and the details can be momentarily forgotten.

Details ... details ... details ... it's all about the details for me!

We push that all the time through the team as well. Get the details right. Get them right, and we are more than halfway towards winning.

My Achilles was so stiff and pinchy on the Saturday morning.

There were less than eight hours to go to the Heineken Cup final. I felt like kicking myself, but I was still in bed, and first thing I had to do was get out of bed and start walking. The Achilles was really nipping hard!

All season long, I'd worn a special boot at night time which helped with the Achilles tendon. It was specially made for me but I hadn't bothered bringing it to Cardiff. Actually, worse than that, I had made the conscious decision not to bring the boot. Carrying it on board with me in my belongings felt like too much of a statement that I was not 100 per cent fit – so I said to myself I wouldn't do that.

It's the little things. I'm always telling myself, and telling others, that it's the littlest things which make the difference between winning and losing.

The rest of the morning was just another morning, surrounded by management and team-mates, in a strange hotel.

As usual, it was mostly about killing time.

Going for a walk.

Taking a rub.

Stretching.

Killing more time.

Eating something.

Going back to my bedroom.

Reading the team sheets.

Heading down to the foyer.

Popping into the team room.

Another bite to eat.

Wandering around.

Sitting down.

And, walking through some of our plays!

There was a nice indoor facility in the Vale of Glamorgan, but it is always too easy for things to look bad when you walk through these plays because some lads are jogging, and some lads are barely jogging. The best thing about the walk-through is that it gets everyone out of the hotel together for a break.

There were still a few hours to go, but my mind was racing. I lay down on my bed, but there was no chance of sleeping. I went down to the team room. Got strapped.

Then, I listened to some music.

My music!

A little Coldplay.

Arcade Fire.

Mumford and Sons …'Little Lion Man'.

'Sweet Disposition' … Temper Trap.

Florence and the Machine.

Snow Patrol.

The National ... 'Fake Empire'.

Cheiks loved to hand us out DVDs with all sorts of emotional images and stirring music on them. He was a believer in the power of imagery and words.

Joe's not so much into that stuff!

Cheiks had the walls of our training camp in Riverview covered with different murals at different times – mountains, soldiers. But Joe has cleaned all of those off!

Joe likes his detail.

Same as me, really.

'...And every occasion
I'll be ready for the funeral
Every occasion once more
It's called the funeral...'

Band of Horses' song 'The Funeral' was a regular on Cheiks' DVDs, and I've kept that music with me through the season.

Every morning.

Every game.

I listen to it over and over.

'Every occasion
Oh, I'm ready for the funeral
And every occasion
Of one billion day funeral...'

I'd been in both dressing rooms in the Millennium Stadium, several times, but it's still a little disorientating and confusing.

My first Six Nations start for Ireland I was in the 'away' dressing room – and 'away' dressing rooms are, obviously, made to be less roomy, slightly less homely than the 'home' dressing room in all big rugby grounds.

But I'd also been in the 'home' dressing room with Ireland.

I don't know, maybe Wales changed them around.

This time we were back in the 'away' dressing room which is now the 'home' dressing room, I think!

I had my strapping done.

My lineout notes were on the wrapping on my wrists. I did them back in the hotel. Always do.

The Millennium Stadium looked as magnificent as ever. It's unlike any other stadium in Ireland or Britain. It's the best.

The roof?

Closed alright!

We all looked up at it, like a bunch of lads arriving in a big city for the first time, arching our backs to see the tops of the skyscrapers!

The dressing room was laid out for us just right.

The touch of Johnny O'Hagan is always there for us, in the preparation of any dressing room we have to enter. Johnny had been meticulous in his work in the Millennium Stadium.

There were Leinster touches, Leinster photos, Leinster messages... Everywhere! *Good man Johnny!*

We always sit in the same places.

That means I'm between Hinesy and Mike Ross.

But when we sat down, I was surprised, for some reason, at how big the dressing rooms in the Millennium Stadium always are and, as a result, lads on the other side of the room seemed a hundred yards away from us!

Lads looked a bit all over the place doing their bits and pieces, and that worried me. Everyone looked to be locked into their own heads.

The room was not buzzed.

It was quiet.

With the team mood feeling that little bit flat for the previous 24 hours, that quietness, and the acres of space worried me. But, I kept reminding myself that if everyone kept their heads on the detail, then, we'd be okay.

We'd be fine.

Mainly I was thinking of the lineout.

I wasn't thinking of the scrum at all!

Get the line-out detail right.

... get set in defence.

Hartley had won the toss.

They chose to kick-off.

I'd have chosen to kick-off if we'd won, but, instead, I got to pick ends.

With the roof closed tightly, there was nothing else to worry about. I looked around the stadium, and it seemed to me that there were more Leinster supporters down at the other end. I decided that we'd run into the noise and colour of our supporters in the second half.

Better to 'run into' them if we need to be sure of scoring!

"This end," I said... "We'll defend this end!"

Only later, long after the game, did it dawn on me that 49 out of the 55 points in the 2011 Heineken Cup final were scored at that 'end'.

Jonny Sexton got 28 of those points, in one of the most amazing individual performances by any player in the tournament's rich history, adding 22 points in the second half to his two first-half penalty goals.

Northampton didn't score in the second half – same as they had failed to score against Leicester in the second half of their Premiership semi-final a week earlier!

More than anything else, the 2011 Heineken Cup final was a 'Game of Scrums', and perhaps a game which is best viewed through those 18 scrums.

3 Minutes

Scrum 1 (Leinster ball):

Deep in our half.

The ball came in.

Cian and I felt the weight from their tight-head side.

Straussy was under a bit of pressure on my right shoulder ... the weight came across my right side.

Jamie was out!

He made a few good yards ... but...

He was carrying one-handed... Wilson got him!

Knock-on.

Leinster 0 : 0 Northampton

4 Minutes

Scrum 2 (Northampton ball):

They went for a push straightaway.

They wanted to take us on.

Wilson picked.

He off-loaded to Dowson.

Leinster 0 : 0 Northampton

6 Minutes

Scrum 3 (Northampton ball):

Inside our 22 ... Sexto whacked the ball.

The biggest kick I'd ever seen from Sexto.

Thought it might go into touch.

But ... the ball rolled on ...

... and went dead!

Their scrum.

Inside our 22.

Tonga'uiha and Hartley went at Mike and Straussy!

I wanted Cian to stay square.

Wanted him to take Mujati on.

Mujati's sheered him off the side.

They were tight ... compact.

They were heavy ... they felt strong!

Romain Poite signalled for a penalty!

They played on...
Attacked the blind side!
Somebody held Shaggy's leg.
I couldn't get over there ... too many bodies were in my way ... and ...
I slipped.
I saw the ball go by me.
Clark had it ... Dowson went over!
Myler converted!
Leinster 0 : 7 Northampton

9 Minutes
Scrum 4 (Leinster ball):

Their 22.
Our put-in!
We looked flat ... still!
They were rushing into everything.
We were slow ... into everything.
They were winning the little battles in every collision.
In amongst us all the time.
They had us rattled.
We needed to settle.
We were better on our own ball.
Mike locked it down well ... but we still felt...
... their weight!
Jamie came under pressure.
He picked quickly.
Leinster 0 : 7 Northampton

11 Minutes
Scrum 5 (Northampton ball):

Darce knocked on.
Poite re-set the scrum.

Cian was okay ... he was good!

We got the shove on.

"Green three ... not straight!" Poite shouted.

Wilson stepped inside Kev McLaughlin.

Jamie tackled him.

Shaggy stole it.

He fed Seanie.

Clark gave up a penalty.

Sexto kicked it!

Leinster 3 : 7 Northampton

18 Minutes

Scrum 6 (Northampton ball):

Knock on ...

... Straussy!

Mike was under big pressure.

We were standing up.

They were walking us.

"Three ... BLUE!" shouted Poite.

Tonga'uiha had Mike under pressure.

Penalty.

We'd looked at this ... we'd seen the footage!

We'd talked this through.

All the time ... every game ... Hartley arrows up!

He stands up ... but, once Poite sees them going forward, that's all he wants to see!

Poite will give the team going forward the verdict all day long.

Myler kicked it.

Leinster 3 : 10 Northampton

23 Minutes

Scrum 7 (Northampton ball):

Drico was through!

Our line-out worked a dream!

We'd planned this with Seanie at scrum-half.

He put Drico away.

We were off and running.

Foden tackled Drico.

Brian tried to get the ball out of the tackle ... but ...

... knocked on!

Scrum was re-set.

They were marching us.

Poite was having none of it ... his arm shot up again ...

... penalty to them!

Leinster 3 : 10 Northampton

27 Minutes

Scrum 8 (Northampton ball):

Mujati pulled on Cian's jersey.

He was binned.

Tom Mercey replaced Mujati.

Clark went off.

Downey moved to openside.

They stood up.

Again.

Again, they walked us!

I turned to Poite.

"They come up..." I shouted at him...

"... and then they're fucking pushing through!"

Poite didn't care.

"Your team is coming under pressure..." he told me.

"... speak to your players!" he ordered.

We could not push!

But Poite was not listening to me.

I wanted to keep talking to him.

I wanted to waste time.
He was not listening to me.
I told him if he doesn't sort this ...
"... there'll be trouble!"
We needed to get into the dressing room.
Cian and I were still pushing into thin air.
We were on the outside of Mercey!
Mercey was doing a good job...
Mercey was a better player than I thought he was!
Hartley had his head into Straussy's face.
We were being beaten up.
They were fired-up.
All their backs were in.
Whooping!
Hollering!
Our front three looked in bad shape.
They were taking a pounding.
Myler kicked them down the field.
Leinster 3 : 10 Northampton

31 Minutes
Scrum 9 (Leinster ball):

Lukey tackled Lawes.
Knock-on!
Our put-in ... and we were doing fine on our put-ins.
Straussy made his strike.
It banged off Cian's knee!
The ball popped back to their side ...
... hit their back line.
They were moving.
They were patient ...
... taking it through phases.
Foden broke past Drico.

He went over.
Myler kicked!
Leinster 3 : 17 Northampton

38 Minutes
Scrum 10 (Northampton ball):

More errors.
Sill under pressure.
Felt like we had a man down, not them!
Mujati and Clark came back onto the field.
"N ... R ... G ... Boys," screamed Hartley!
We felt strong...
... stayed square!
This time ... there was no second shove from them.
They had the ball out.
They moved through the phases again.
Hartley got the ball.
He broke through in the right corner.
Poite went to the TMO.
"He's scored!" said Jamie.
"He's got it," said Darce!
Poite raised his arm.
Myler took forever.
Myler kicked the conversion ... finally.
The ball bounced off the post.
Leinster 6 : 22 Northampton

Second Half
46 Minutes
Scrum 11 (Northampton ball):

Cian knocked-on.
Sexto had already scored our first try.

Jamie took Mujati out of it.

Sexto left Tonga'uiha for dead on his inside.

Sexto kicked the conversion!

We needed to score fast.

Ten or 15 minutes without scoring ... and what would Northampton think?

What'll they start doing?

We needed to obliterate the first half.

We'd turned them over from the opening restart!

Sexto was a man possessed.

Seanie was carrying.

Jamie was carrying.

We were all holding onto the ball.

Jenno was talking and talking ... and he was hitting.

Tails were up.

We knew we had time.

We could score points!

We could see holes!

We knew we had our scrum back!

Feekie's words were in everyone's heads!

Mike was a new man.

Straussy was a new man.

Cian and I were in the scrum ... getting some work done.

Finally!

Rock solid!

Wilson picked and fed Dickson.

Clarke got the ball.

Jenno and Jamie made a double hit.

Leinster 13 : 22 Northampton

51 Minutes

Scrum 12 (Leinster ball):

Darce was held up over the line.

Scrum Five!

Mike couldn't wait to get into Tonga'uiha!

We were carrying the ball.

Pounding away.

We were moving it.

Sexto went through Clarke ... Jamie blocked Dowson.

Wraparound!

Sexto ... second try.

Sexto converted!

We had too much expectation in the first half.

Not enough fear.

We had nine handling errors in the first half.

Eight missed tackles in the first half.

We could not hold onto the ball ... in the first half.

Too pressurised!

In the second half ... they were pressurised.

They wanted to celebrate at half time.

They didn't want to play the second half.

We knew they'd tire.

They were tiring fast!

Leinster 20 : 22 Northampton

55 Minutes

Scrum 13 (Leinster ball):

Foden knocked on.

Mike, Straussy and Cian took the hit!

They stayed square.

Strong as a house!

Their front row was up.

We walked them back.

Poite was happy.

Poite put his arm up.

The Leinster supporters went nuts.

The Millennium Stadium turned blue.

We believed.

We wanted to steamroll them.

The tables had turned.

Completely turned!

Our backs were in!

Whooping...

... Hollering!

Mike looked like he might cry with happiness!

Mike deserved this ... he'd taken his pounding...

But Mike had come back for revenge!

Mike would never walk away!

In the scrum ... it's personal for Mike.

Mike's our man ... our specialist ... our hero!

Sexto kicked the penalty.

Seventeen points!

In seventeen minutes!

Leinster 23 : 22 Northampton

63 Minutes

Scrum 14 (Leinster ball):

Hartley was sucking in the air.

He was feeling it!

Dowson was in the sin-bin...

... They were back to 14 men again.

Sexto had kicked another penalty.

They buckled ...

... they were nearly broken.

Wilson went off bloodied and sorry-looking.

We could see it in their faces.

They were bloodied.

And bowed!

And bashed!

Cian went off!

Heinke sent Mujati skywards.
Poite put his arm in the air.
Advantage.
Jamie charged upfield.
Seanie.
Straussy.
I dived ...
... held the ball by my fingertips.
Hinesy went over!
Try!
Sexto converted.
Leinster 33 : 22 Northampton

68 Minutes
Scrum 15 (Northampton ball):

Hartley had gone!
Heinke got the shove on.
Scrappy ball.
Foden collected.
Ashton received!
He looked beaten ... done!
Isa tackled ...
... Ashton was nearly gone!
Breakdown.
We won the ball.
Game began to fizzle out.
Game was nearly gone too!
We then began to fizzle out.
Leinster supporters were singing.
We needed to play to the final whistle!
We need to keep playing.
Leinster 33 : 22 Northampton

73 Minutes
Scrum 16 (Northampton ball):

Wake up.
A wake up call for us.
They got the shove on us ... again!
We got bulldozed.
Easy for Poite.
Penalty.
They tapped!
And went!
Leinster 33 : 22 Northampton

77 Minutes
Scrum 17 (Leinster ball):

We were left defending.
Their last push.
They looked desperate.
They were gone!
All gone!
They found pressure from somewhere.
Stan had come in!
I could see Stan smiling.
Stan was loving it!
Jamie moved quickly with the ball.
Leinster 33 : 22 Northampton

78 Minutes
Scrum 18 (Leinster ball):

Their last ounce of energy.
We were defending again.
Also ... we're celebrating.

We were ... Heineken Cup champions.

Against Leicester in '09 ... we had to defend ... to the death!

Not in the 2011 Heineken Cup final!

Leinster 33 : 22 Northampton

We brought Northampton, in the twenty minutes after half time, to a place where they'd never been before. We'd spoken about that, about bringing them to that place!

We'd planned to bring them there in the first half!

The physical, and mental, pressure which bore down on them in the second half quickly over-powered them.

The 2011 Heineken Cup final will either destroy Northampton as a team, or prove to be the final learning curve for them.

I think it will be the latter.

When a team wins something, it's all about getting the right people to represent the team at that supreme and memorable moment. Once the final whistle had gone in Cardiff, I had Darce and Shaggy in my head.

Shaggy had had such a tough year with injury, and he's also been such a leader in our dressing room. He's been so courageous.

Darce is made of stone, and Leinster has built so much on his shoulders!

As the medal presentation began, I told the two of them to hold back and stay with me!

When, at the very end of the presentation ceremony, my name was announced as captain, the three of us walked up onto the rostrum together. We shook hands with the officials.

I went behind the trophy.

Darce and Shaggy stood either side of it ... and I shouted ... "One ... Two ... THREE!" The Heineken Cup was lifted high into the air.

But only the match squad was on the field! In Murrayfield, we'd been able to get our entire squad – everyone who'd played every minute of every game that whole season – into the middle of the celebration.

This time, the ERC guys weren't having that!

"Get all the lads out here!" shouted someone behind me, but it was impossible. The presentation was about to start and the rest of our squad, in their team suits, were pinned into their section of the ground by a ring of stewards.

I felt disappointed about that.

But, I couldn't delay the presentation.

Once it was over, I ran to where the lads were pegged in ... and, I'm not the sort of character who dives into groups of people but ... incredibly ... I dived into the arms of all the lads.

There was mayhem.

The lads had flown over that morning. They'd had a few beers waiting for the game, and they were mad to get out onto the field and join us for the real celebrations. As a small riot began to erupt, the security guards did the decent thing and parted to let everyone out onto the field.

My dad, Frank was out there, too!

He'd got his hands on a pass, as he did in Murrayfield after the '09 final, and we found each other and hugged. For both of us, it was the greatest moment of my rugby life!

I found Dairine too ... my wife-to-be two weeks later!

We kissed quickly.

Earlier, I had also found Dylan Hartley, sitting on his own on the ground near one touchline, and said my few words to him.

"Well done ... best of luck in the future!"

There's nothing more I could have said.

I found it hard to hold back my delight. A minute earlier, the whole team had grouped together in the centre of the field, and danced and jumped up and down... 'I Gotta Feeling' from the Black Eyed Peas blaring all around us.

I was the happiest man in that magnificent stadium.

Back in the dressing room, back in the room where we'd been just under an hour earlier at half time, wondering if we'd blown it, and telling one another how we'd got 40 minutes to save our season, there was absolute joy.

The same room ... the same team ... and the Heineken Cup!

I didn't want to leave the room.

In Murrayfield, two years earlier, I'd got a clash of heads during the game and, immediately after the medal presentations, I had to go to the medical room and get half a dozen stitches in my head.

It seemed to take ages.

By the time I got back to the dressing room, I felt that a special moment in my life had passed me by! Then, I was gone again, for the press conference. I remember only seeing the team, and seeing the team celebrating, in snatches.

I wanted to stay in the dressing room in Cardiff ... forever!

This time, I wasn't moving for anybody ... not for a long time!

Quickly, very quickly indeed, the Heineken Cup, the trophy itself, becomes a poisoned chalice.

Outside the ground.

Getting on the team coach ... getting off the team coach!

Getting into Cardiff airport.

Arriving in Dublin airport.

Getting on the team coach ... arriving at the Burlington Hotel!

Everyone wants to touch it.

Everyone wants to pat the back of the man who's holding it.

Everyone wants a photograph of it.

Pat Kenny got his chance at the airport, but got drowned in beer for his troubles!

I kept spinning the trophy off to other players every 10 minutes, but it kept coming back to me!

Luckily, I had it in my hands when I hugged my sister, Sarah, in Dublin airport, and I popped her new-born son, Fionn, into the cup for a very special family photo.

In the hotel, I spent some fantastic, happy hours with my family, my friends, my coach Joe Schmidt, my old team-mates ... and Felipe Contepomi!

By 3am we were entering a nightclub in the city centre!

By 5am I headed to The Bank bar on College Green!

The team had broken up through the early hours. I was with my close mates – my Best Man at my wedding the following month, David Chawke, owned the place.

The streets of the city centre were now ghostly quiet.

There were steel barricades everywhere.

Gardai everywhere … in the earliest hours of the morning!

I didn't know what was happening.

A few of us got in through the front door of Dave's pub. We didn't know that a few Gardai had spotted us.

Myself and Ciaran Scally, my friend, and my former team-mate, sat down for a quiet pint at one of the tables. And Ciaran, it's fair to say at this stage of his life, has put on a little bit of weight since his own playing days! A couple of the Gardai appeared in the door.

"What's going on in here?" they asked … "Obama's coming in today … who's in here?"

Dave was talking to them.

He turned and pointed at me, telling the Gardai … "That's Leo Cullen!"

Then, he pointed at Ciaran Scally, and told the same Gardai … "And … that there … that's Mike Ross!"

The Gardai seemed happy enough, and left.

Dave closed the door and came over to us.

"I thought," he said, "they'd like to meet two Leinster heroes!"

Heineken Cup
Final
Millennium Stadium, Cardiff
May 21, 2011

Leinster 33, Northampton 22

HT: Leinster 6, Northampton 22
Attendance: 72,456
Man of the Match: Jonny Sexton
Referee: Romain Poite (France)

—∿∿—

Scoring sequence – 7 Mins: Dowson try, Myler con 0-7; **14:** Sexton pen 3-7;
21: Myler pen 3-10; **31:** Foden try, Myler con 3-17; **36:** Sexton pen; **38:** Hartley try.
Half time: 6-22; 45: Sexton try, con 13-22; **53:** Sexton try, con 20-22; **57:** Sexton pen 23-22;
61: Sexton pen 26-22; **66:** Hines try, Sexton con 33-22

Leinster: I Nacewa; S Horgan, B O'Driscoll, G D'Arcy (F McFadden 67), L Fitzgerald; J Sexton
(I Madigan 78), E Reddan (I Boss 72): C Healy (H van der Merwe 61), R Strauss (J Harris-
Wright 79), M Ross (S Wright 78), L Cullen Capt., N Hines (D Toner 78), K McLaughlin
(Jennings HT), S O'Brien, J Heaslip.

Northampton: B Foden; C Ashton (S Commins 78), J Clarke , J Downey (J Ansbro 66),
P Diggin; S Myler (S Geraghty 66), L Dickson; S Tonga'uiha (A Waller 66), D Hartley Capt.
(B Sharman 69), B Mujati (Mercey 66), C Lawes, C Day (M Sorenson 78), C Clark (Mercey
28-36), P Dowson, R Wilson (M Easter 63). Sin-binned: B Mujati (26-36), P Dowson (59-69)

EPILOGUE

One week after the Heineken Cup final, on May 28, we lost to Munster in the final of the Magners League in Thomond Park. It was 19-9.

They were fired-up.

We tried to fire ourselves up, but we didn't have enough players in the game. Too many Leinster players didn't turn up, and a pushover try at the very end rubbed salt into our wounds.

The day after winning the Heineken Cup in the Millennium Stadium, we had a memorable 'homecoming' in the RDS on the Sunday afternoon. It was agreed that we should all go out for a 'team celebration' that evening, take Monday as a day off, and then get our heads into the League final on the Tuesday morning.

It was a sensible plan.

Better to get the celebrations done and dusted and then clear our heads and think of Munster. Sunday night and Monday night were great. On Tuesday morning, everybody was ready to get back down to business.

At the start of that session on the Tuesday morning, I got an unmerciful bang on my neck while doing a wrestling drill, which did my mood no good after a few nights out. We trained hard that day in an effort to make sure the lads had got all of the celebrations fully out of their system.

On and off throughout the season, I had been getting 'stingers', for the first time in my whole career. A stinger is an unpleasant experience, to put it mildly, and I'm not exactly sure what causes them, or what happens to your body when you get that sort of bang. My theory is that the nerve roots have narrowed a bit and then, when the nerve becomes inflamed after getting a bang, it sends a shock down your arm. It can leave your arm numb and de-powered.

I got five or six stingers in total during the last couple of months of the season and, each time, I was back to normal and feeling okay after a few minutes. But, that Tuesday morning, I was in no mood for the damn thing. We didn't want to talk-up the Munster match too early in the week. It was better that we should 'flick the switch' in the second half of the week instead, when minds would be 100 per cent concentrated.

I had my ideas of how to do that.

It was clear that it was going to be an emotional occasion for Munster. They were signing off on a disappointing season, which would have been doubly or trebly disappointing if they were party to us winning the Heineken Cup and the Magners League title!

We were the underdogs with most neutral parties, and I had no problem playing that up. They were playing in their home ground and I informed the media that the ball was in Munster's court.

We needed to gather ourselves together, and be absolutely prepared for everything which Munster were going to throw at us. I also wanted to play on the sense of friendship and comradeship which had intensified so brilliantly in the Leinster dressing room over the previous three years, and which directly led to us winning the Heineken Cup, twice.

Stan Wright was a powerful force in the winning of our first Heineken Cup in 2009. Nathan Hines, similarly, was a tower of strength in his two short years with us and had a big hand, from start to finish, in our second Heineken Cup campaign.

Stan and Hinesy were both on their way out of the club. Stan was joining up with Michael Cheika in Stade Francais, and Hinesy was heading further south and teaming up with Clermont.

In Leinster, we would never usually have a team meeting the night before a game, but for the League final we decided to do things differently. Joe wanted us to stay overnight in Limerick the night before the game and I wanted to have a players' meeting. All the players in a room together.

And just the players!

After I opened the meeting, I handed over to the two boys and asked Stan and Hinesy to do the talking. Hinesy spoke first, and he found it hard, breaking down a little before he could get a word out. Stan followed him. He too struggled to finish what he wanted to say. There was a huge charge in the room listening to the two boys.

Everybody was emotional.

At the end of the night, the emotion was calmed when Stan Wright was formally christened 'Snot Bubble' by his team-mates. But, it had been one of the most electrifying team meetings I had ever been involved in through all my years with Leinster.

The week had been long and brilliant, but it had also been draining. We ran out of steam in the last 20 minutes against Munster, and nobody beats Munster, especially in Thomond Park, by playing for just 60 minutes of the game.

They had all guns blazing, right to the bitter end. But, as a team, they also had David Wallace playing his 200th game for his province. At the time, it looked like John Hayes was playing his last game in a red shirt, and all of his family were there. Also, Alan Quinlan was retiring after a lifetime as the team's enforcer in the back row. All of this was in the mix.

With or without all of those motivating factors, Munster might have won. They were thoroughly deserving champions on the night, beating us by three tries to nil. And, in the old days, they would have been crowned League champions some weeks earlier as they actually topped the table with 13 points to spare, having won 21 of their 24 matches in the regular season.

With 15 minutes left in the game, we led 9-7, thanks to three penalty goals from Jonny, and at times, especially at the start of the second half, we had dominated them and looked determined to take the League title home with us. After Doug Howlett had opened the scoring with a try in the 12th minute, we had kept them scoreless for 54 minutes. Keith Earls scored their second try in the 66th minute, and, one minute from the end, Nigel Owens awarded them a penalty try.

There was not enough fight – and insufficient resistance – from us in those final 15 minutes. It was Munster's night!

And, as they celebrated on the field, they honoured Paul Darbyshire by presenting him with the cup. Paul was Munster's former head of strength and conditioning and he was in a wheelchair, in the final stages of battling a terrible illness. He had been diagnosed with motor neurone disease just the previous September. He passed away, peacefully in his sleep, just one month after the final, leaving behind his wife, Lyndsay and their four children.

We were back in the Burlington Hotel on the Sunday night and I was in fairly brutal form. A week which had commenced at an unbelievable high had ended with us getting hit on the chin by Munster with a penalty try. I didn't want to be in a bad mood. But I could not lift myself. I didn't feel like drinking or partying. I was not much different to everyone else around me, except, I was in an extra bad mood… Because I was in a bad mood! I didn't want to feel like that.

The following Saturday, Dairine and I were getting married. Within a fourteen-day period, I would have the honour of leading Leinster to a second Heineken Cup, and making myself the happiest man in the whole province of Leinster by marrying Dairine Kennedy.

What more could a man ask for?

The problem was, in between, we had been beaten by Munster in Thomond Park. It was the second time to lose to them down there in successive months, and it hurt. I had to get Munster out of my head, as fast as humanly possible. So, on the Monday, I led the Leinster team on a day and a night of complete and unrivalled celebration.

St Brigid's Church in Kilrush was as imposing and awe-inspiring as any rugby stadium I have ever entered, when I got there (at 2.36pm exactly, according to members of the local press!) on Saturday, June 4, and waited for Dairine to arrive. I had good company, with David Chawke, Tom Keating and Owen, my brother, as groomsmen.

Father Joe Power, the Parish Priest, and some of the local people were brilliant, and had erected giant banners outside the church to welcome the entire Leinster team.

I was confident Dairine would arrive!

Our wedding was timed for 3pm and, as is the bride's right, Dairine left me waiting beyond the appointed hour. Not that it was entirely my bride's decision, as she had chosen to make the journey from her home in a magnificent 45-year-old Jaguar, which conked out about 200 yards from the church. Rather than walk, my bride then waited in the car until a second car arrived to end the distress.

Dairine looked incredibly beautiful in an ivory white dress. Her bridesmaids – her sister, Kiera, Louise Bloomer and Cliona Godwin – all looked beautiful, and wore blue.

It was a magnificent, sunny day, with perfect blue skies. Dairine and I had no idea how happy we would be with our day. And that surprised me a little, I have to admit. I was not expecting to be as nervous as I was in the church, or before making my speech later in the evening.

I loved every second of the day.

It was perfection.

If anybody had told me that my wedding day would eclipse the greatest days of my rugby career, I would have had trouble believing them, but it did. It was a day on an entirely different level altogether.

Dairine and I were in good hands, because some of the safest pairs of hands I could have found were on 'duty' around the church.

My Uncle Liam, my dad's brother, was there to inform the local journalists and photographers, who had turned out in flattering numbers, who was who amongst our guests.

My dad, Frank, was also at his brother's shoulder to fill in any of the blank spaces, and also to proudly let it be known to the local media that it was a particularly happy month for the Cullen family – not because the Heineken Cup had been reclaimed two weeks earlier but, far more importantly, because a first grandchild to him and my mum, Paula, had been born a month earlier. Little Fionn was present with his mother, my sister, Sarah, and her husband, John.

Bob Casey, my lifelong friend since our days in school in Blackrock, was also on duty (again, according to the local press, Bob was in charge of

'Security and Photo Opportunities'!)

The wedding ceremony went smoothly and as planned, then, that evening, everyone retired to the Kennedy home where a magnificent marquee greeted guests and housed our wedding reception. The following day we all enjoyed a sumptuous barbecue, and we ended up in Treacy's in Enniscorthy for a 'pig on a spit'. The next day we checked into the Monart Hotel and Spa, which is owned by the former Wexford All-Ireland winning manager, Liam Griffin. On the Wednesday morning, my wife and I flew to Italy for our honeymoon.

On Monday afternoon, in the Monart, I was busying myself checking through our bags in our bedroom. Dairine had already headed down to the fantastic spa which they have there, and I told her I'd join her in ten minutes.

I received a text on my phone.

It was not a text message which I had expected, and I was suprised by the number and the name. The text was from Ronan O'Donnell, Leinster's Operations Manager.

What's Ronan want? I thought.

I looked at it. At first I was slightly confused. But, I read the text a second time. It read ... "Leinster, Bath, Glasgow, Montpellier."

I'd completely forgotten that the draw for the 2011-12 Heineken Cup had been made that same day.

Bath ...

... Glasgow ...

... and Montpellier!

My brain started getting into gear all over again.

In August, 2011, I became the 100th person to captain Ireland, when I was chosen by Declan Kidney to lead Ireland out in the first of the team's

World Cup warm-up matches in Murrayfield.

It was an honour way outside of my dreams.

Deccie also asked me to captain Ireland in the second warm-up game in Bordeaux against France, and then, the following week, I captained an Ireland XV against Connacht.

At the third time of trying, I was selected for the Irish squad for the World Cup, in New Zealand, and I captained the team against Russia. We defeated Russia, 62-12, in Rotorua, on our way to winning all of the games in our group which contained one of the pre-tournament favourites, Australia.